The Sea Gull

A DRAMA IN FOUR ACTS

Translated from the Russian of
ANTON CHEKHOV

by
STARK YOUNG

SAMUEL FRENCH, INC.
45 WEST 25TH STREET   NEW YORK 10010
7623 SUNSET BOULEVARD HOLLYWOOD 90046
LONDON   TORONTO

Plays translated by Stark Young

The Sea Gull . . . . Chekhov
Le Légataire universel . . . Regnard
Georges Dandin . . . . Molière
La Mandragola . . . . . . Machiavelli
The Cherry Orchard . . . . . Chekhov
The Three Sisters . . . . Chekhov

The Sea Gull

CONTENTS

PREFACE — vii

BIOGRAPHICAL NOTE — xxxviii

TRANSLATIONS OF THE SEA GULL — xl

CHARACTERS IN THE PLAY — xli

THEATRE PROGRAM — xlii

THE SEA GULL — 3

NOTES FOR ACTORS — 63

PREFACE

TRANSLATING THE SEA GULL

The play in this volume is a translation, it is not an adaptation. No speech has been moved out of the place where Chekhov put it and, with the exception here and there of little odds and ends that might come to three or four lines, nothing has been cut.

With so many translations available, we could scarcely pretend that Chekhov's meanings as a rule are not easy to discover. Theoretically, at least, it might have been a good thing to retain as much from earlier versions of *The Sea Gull* as might still seem workable, thus leaving undisturbed whatever familiarity with the play there was, and treating Chekhov rather as if he had written in English. I made no effort to retain these former renderings. But, on the other hand, I made no effort to avoid them. Where the Russian of a passage could mean one thing and nothing else, I felt no temptation merely to be different. There was plenty to change without that. A more insistent problem at the moment is how I shall talk about translating *The Sea Gull* and not seem bent on merely disparaging the other translations and endorsing my own. It would be too bad if I should seem so, for this essay is not written for any version's sake, but wholly in defense of Chekhov.

Having made this translation, I find myself in a peculiar position. On one hand there have been Doctor

Nicholas Rumanceff, for thirty years a member of the
Moscow Art Theatre, sometime chairman of its Board
of Directors, and a renowned scholar and man of letters;
Madame Maria Ouspenskaya, formerly of the Moscow
Art Theatre, one of its finest actresses, as she has been
one of ours these last twelve years; Mrs. Catherine
Burland, a Russian lady living in America and brilliantly
read in the literature of both countries; and various other
cultivated Russians, who hailed my translation as being
so like Chekhov.

What they have said is all by happy chance in Doctor
Rumanceff's note:

"After reading the reviews I might have concluded
that *The Sea Gull* had been rearranged for a better
understanding and response on the part of American
audiences. Knowing the other translations and knowing
the play, I could easily have believed that this new version, to be thus successful, must be an adaptation. But
such was not the case. I found almost word for word
Chekhov's characteristic, it seemed to me, in Mr.
Young's translation. The reason the American public
loves and understands the play is because it is like Chekhov in English."

On the other hand there have been a good number of
my friends, many correspondents known and unknown
to me personally, and several critics, who praised my
translation because it is so unlike Chekhov—what they
say virtually amounts to that, though they never quite
say it in so many words. Some of these do not bring in
Chekhov at all by way of comparison with my effort
(which in a way is sensible and just, so long as one does
not read Russian); they merely express their own pleasure in the play my translation has brought them. Others
speak from a considerable judgment, gathered one way
and another, as to what Chekhov is. These comments,
however, are related not so much to Chekhov as to the
conception of Chekhov that has gradually been built up
by the translations and productions in English.

I might discuss this matter of Chekhov's Russian script of *The Sea Gull* as compared with the accepted translations till doomsday, and people could take it or leave it, as after all only one man's opinion. They might, if they chose, suspect me of taking cover behind the comparative strangeness of the language to say anything I have a mind to, while I on my part could scarcely expect them to do me the justice of checking my points and arguments with the original. On that ground, then, I might talk my head off and all I said might forever seem to them very little more than theory.

The alternative would be some sort of record, point by point, case upon case, a kind of certified list, as it were, that would show how and where the divers translation of this one play may have failed Chekhov. I will try to set down enough of my observations to give the reader something of the shock that came to me when I first saw more or less what Chekhov was like. And perhaps he will feel some of the dismay I felt when the thought struck me about the other plays, *Uncle Vanya, Three Sisters, The Cherry Orchard:* how opaque are the translations of them that we have taken for granted?

I hope not to sound unfair or ungrateful when I say that the most useful method of showing what the Chekhov is seems to be that of citing from the translations examples of what it is not. If I could do these notes really well, they would upset the whole tradition of Chekhov in English, and cause new translations to be made of all his other plays.

In all the seven translations of *The Sea Gull* that I have read, the general meanings are, of course, about the same; the difference lies in the words, the structure, the tone, which means that, by just so much, a different thing has been said. This kind of difference appears between, for example, the two following paragraphs, both versions of a speech of Constantine's in ACT I. They are like and unlike enough to make you wonder as to the difference between either of them and what Chekhov actually wrote, and so will serve for a start.

I

"I love my mother, I love her devotedly, but I think she leads a stupid life. She always has this man of letters of hers on her mind, and the newspapers are always frightening her to death, and I am tired of it. Plain, human egoism sometimes speaks in my heart, and I regret that my mother is a famous actress. If she were an ordinary woman I think I should be a happier man. What could be more intolerable and foolish than my position, Uncle, when I find myself the only nonentity among a crowd of her guests, all celebrated authors and artists? I feel that they only endure me because I am her son. Personally, I am nothing, nobody."

II

"I love my mother—I love her very much—but she leads a senseless sort of life, always taken up with this literary gentleman, her name is always trotted out in the papers—and that wearies me. And sometimes the simple egoism of an ordinary mortal makes me feel sorry that my mother is a celebrated actress, and I fancy that if she were an ordinary woman I should be happier. Uncle, what could be more hopeless and stupid than my position? She used to have visitors, all celebrities—artists and authors—and among them all I was the only one who was nothing, and they put up with me because I was her son. Who am I? What am I?"

In No. II, from Mrs. Garnett's translation, except for the phrase "literary gentlemen," which is highly sarcastic and not what Chekhov says, we keep close to the meaning. No. I, by Mrs. Fell, has, as theatre writing, a certain air of energy and convincingness. This only serves to carry us still farther astray in a translation where otherwise almost every other word implies some fantastic distinction or subtlety that Chekhov never dreamt of. Here, for one instance, we have as hero a young man who is plainly both tragic and voluble, as well as articulate and unexpected to a degree. He loves his mother devotedly but thinks her life stupid, with her man of letters always on her mind. And this must be the reason —this having a man of letters on her mind—why she could be so much frightened by the newspapers, and her son is tired of that. And yet his egoism speaks in his heart—a figure of speech with a curiously subjective lyricism to it—though all he feels about it is "regret" or is such only delicacy of statement? "Personally—" he is able to screen his despair with a casual phrase. The single sentence about an ordinary woman and a happier man suggests somehow modern implications. His sorrows in his mother's *salon* are still going on, even here in the country.

All that astonishing mixture hangs together and fits perfectly into what most of us think Chekhov is like— certainly I once did, for my first acquaintance with Chekhov was through Mrs. Fell's translation.

As a matter of fact, none of those rarities are in the Chekhov at all. Taking his Russian lines, I have followed the steps of provocation, as it were, that the translator met there, and so much more than coped with. The mother's life is not "stupid," it is "meaningless" or "senseless." She has not the author "on her mind," she "fusses over" him, is taken up with him—the same Russian word that applies to women with dogs. The newspapers are not "frightening her to death"; what Trepleff says is that her name is "forever chucked about in the papers—and that irks me." There is no such sentence about an ordinary woman and a happier man, but only a clause, part of a longer and simpler statement; and the word *man* does not occur at all. The point about him and his mother's celebrities is not that it is an ever-present issue but is an old wound kept rankling by his situation. The "Personally, I am nobody, nothing," is all bosh; the line merely asks who is he and what is he?

But even a short speech, one of half a line in fact, can make us wonder about the Chekhov of it. In Act I, for example, when the schoolmaster winds up his well-worn little harangue about his salary and his expenses, the sentence in six of the translations reads these six ways:

"Answer me that, if you can."

"Where does that leave you?"

"There's no getting round that."

"You've got to work mighty hard to do it all."

"It's a tight fit."

"A stiff proposition, isn't it?"

The sentence is there on the first page of the Russian text. Going on, in fact, we find that in ACT IV he repeats it; this time Doctor Dorn beats the schoolmaster to it at the end of the familiar harangue about salary and expenses. None of his translators, however, with one exception—Mr. Koteliansky—has seen this device of Chekhov's, and so we get as many more versions again, all different from the first six and from each other— "You've got to look sharp to make both ends meet," "A hard riddle to solve," "You won't get much change out of that," etc., etc.

That makes eleven versions in all of this one short sentence, and anybody would think there must be something very subtle about it, or elusive, or Slavic or what not, for the translator to contend with. But the dictionary seems to give the sense well enough, and the Russian delicatessen man seems at home with this expression. Вот тут и вертись. He tries to explain it by stirring his hand round and round, quite as we might do if we tried to explain our "chasing your tail" or to explain the phrase "a vicious circle" to him. The idea of it is, "So it just goes round in a circle." Or, "So it just goes round and round."

Even by this time we must be prepared for surprises when we come to Chekhov's own text of *The Sea Gull.*

Our greatest surprise should be in the tone, which in a dramatic work is a diffused and intangible but final quality that reveals its general characteristic. A single page of his own text may be enough to show us how there has been gradually built up for Chekhov in English a tone quite false to him, so that our general conception of him is almost fantastically off the track. This is a great misfortune to our theatre. Chekhov has many qualities that we respond to, naturally and vividly. His technical method is one we cannot only admire but can make use of. He has already been a strong influence among us. He would be a much readier and deeper influence if his true tone could be established.

We shall be surprised too at the number of contrivances in the writing itself, those balances, repetitions for stage effect, repetitions for stage economy, theatrical combinations and devices, time-patterns, and so on, that are the fruits of much intention and technical craft, and that are almost totally absent from the translations— the truth is, if you went by the translations, you would never even suspect Chekhov of such practices.

If the presence of these many contrivances surprises us, we shall be even more surprised at the absence of a quality that most people have come to associate with Chekhov, and that has done a good deal to set him back with the producers. I mean the impression of vagueness, monotony of mood, even of incomprehensibility. We seem to have accepted these traits in *The Sea Gull* as obstacles that an otherwise admirable play has to surmount. Or we admire their results as truly Chekhovian; or welcome it all as Slavic. That last is a fine bit of tosh. Undoubtedly there are emotions, or combinations of emotions, and situations, in *The Sea Gull* that might be called Slavic, but not the lines. The style in this play is easy and clear, never confused or obscure so far as the words go. The structure of the sentences could not be simpler. "How was one to utter these simplest of phrases simply . . .?" the directors at the new theatre wondered. Stanislavsky, the *regisseur* in charge of *The Sea Gull*, went even further: he did not know any way at all to proceed; he found the words too simple. So much, then, for our English theatre and its tradition of Chekhov's moody vagueness.

Producers of *The Sea Gull,* so far as I know, have
usually taken some published version and to varying
extents—sometimes a good deal, sometimes very little—
cut here and there, or transposed bits from other versions
of the play, or wherever they felt the need, written in
words of their own. They hoped thus to clarify the
dialogue, above all they hoped to give it stage naturalness or plausibility as human theatre utterance. And
meanwhile they are ready to believe that the translator of
this play is a hard-pressed man who finds himself in a
quandary between preserving a certain fidelity to Chekhov's text and achieving a certain naturalness in the
translation. It seems to them that very often anybody
could tell by the way the speeches read that they had been
very hard to translate into English with any real accuracy. And I certainly shared once in that opinion. I should
certainly have said that nothing but the most consci-
entious, and almost fanatical, determination to translate
Chekhov's lines exactly would make you write, for
example, this sentence, one of many such:

"Our time is passing, we are no longer young, and if
only we could lay aside concealment and lying for the
end of our lives anyway."

Morally, as it were, such translation as this of Mrs.
Garnett's here is singularly persuasive. The very defects
of its writing help to convince us of its fidelity. And so I
accepted such peculiarities as inextricably bound up with
Chekhov's art; doubtless I put them down to the "Russian soul" and let it go at that, which is what various
other admirers of Chekhov have told me they did. What
Paulina says is much simpler: She merely says that if
only, for the rest of their lives at least, they could stop
hiding, stop pretending.

I should have known all along that Chekhov's lines
would not be diffused or stuffy, studied, elaborate, or
what not. His method, known as the realistic-psycho-
logical, is to take actual material such as we find in life
and manage it in such a way that the inner meanings are

made to appear. On the surface the life in his plays is natural, possible, and in effect at times even casual. It should, if I had had my wits about me, follow, therefore, that the words he uses would be simple or at least familiar or natural, as we find them in our actual life day by day. The depths and subtleties of meaning would, accordingly, not be created through subtle words, difficult phrases, blurred clauses, complex statements, vague lines, or a style of the muggy, symbolic, swing-on-to-your-atmosphere sort. Not through such qualities in the words themselves, but through their management or combination would the inner content appear. But somehow I never suspected that fact.

If I had not expected so many of those contrivances I have spoken of, by which Chekhov increased the sum of life in his play and made his lines meat for actors, I was prepared even less for the open and healthy means by which these devices are contrived. They are not contrived —as the general conception of Chekhov might lead us to think they would be—by intense or hazy or morbid shadings and subtle implications, but with plain technical craft, with marvelous accuracy in the choice of simple terms, and with wit. Almost the first thing I heard Miss Fontanne say after rehearsing the third act of *The Sea Gull*—the finest, most varied and most terrific, in the play—was how witty it is. And she was right. An elusive but wholly robust wit proceeding from within a gentle nature and therefore not inhuman or cruel; pervading all; and giving a vibrant proportion to the whole. It is not unlike Shakespeare's in a kind of sustaining animation that it provides. In *The Nation* not long ago Mr. Joseph Wood Krutch wrote that *The Sea Gull* "is not a mixture of comedy and tragedy. . . . Neither the spirit of tragedy nor the spirit of comedy could include all the variety of incident and character which the play presents. They can only be included within some mood less downright than that of tragedy or comedy, and one of Chekhov's originalities was just his success in creating such a mood." To that keen observation, I should like to add my opinion that in the creation of this particular mood, wit, *per se*, played a great part, the rest being mostly played by Chekhov's lyricism.

Something of the same comment that Mr. Krutch applies to the mood in Chekhov applies also to Chekhov's style. And the wit and lyricism that help determine this style help also to refute certain popular notions of its obscurity. For wit is of all things the very contrary to vagueness ; and lyricism is the poetry, not the confusion, of the feelings.

It is along this line of wit that we discern how *The Sea Gull* partakes of the nature of comedy, and bring ourselves to Chekhov's own classification of the play as "a comedy." In its centrifugal, or objective, aspect, it shows us the individual will and passion set up against what is larger, more nearly whole, et cetera. We are thus reviewing this human scene and struggle from without, from some distance, as it were, and to our final thinking reaction this minor urgency and private commotion falls by sheer contrast into the comic scale.

The wit, however, exists in the conception of the scene. Or to put it another way, we may say that the scene is contained and measured within a witty frame. On the other hand the lines as they move onward, the individual pressure, the immediate surface, all that side of the play is lyric.

The lyricism of *The Sea Gull* is quite as important as the wit, and arises from the contrary motion. It is centripetal and moves from the passionate will or desire down to the individual's center, acceding to whatever measure and cry is felt to be there, bringing it forward, and giving it a kind of trembling clarity. If it were not for this gentle inner excitement that Chekhov feels in their company, his way of making his characters reveal themselves might seem ruthless. As it is, we find underneath the whole of *The Sea Gull* a curious kind of singing life. It is something like this that Nemirovitch-Dantchenko, in that fine book about his experience in the Russian theatre, speaks of as binding him to Chekhov

". . . with such infatuation, I seized upon his poetry, his lyricism, his unanticipated truth." And it is this that leads me to take such pleasure in the fact that Mr. Krutch remarked the "elegiac," as he puts it, note in my translation.

And now my translation of *The Sea Gull* has, among other generous commendations, been praised as "vigorous for modern ears," or as "brightening and shortening the text," or as "agreeably omitting the literal translation of the Russian original and the Russian idiom." And there are those who admire the effort, but take for granted that it represents only some form of accommodation. To their minds my translation will seem, at best, an amiable simplification of complex matters, or, at the worst, a misguided attempt to force the colloquial on to what they have learned to think of as the seriousness and abstraction of the Chekhov mood. But, whatever else my translation may be, it is not an obliging accommodation. How closely it follows the play we have seen from Doctor Rumanceff's comment. As for any simplification, my sorest struggle was to get my lines as simple as Chekhov's—a difficult problem because such simplicity must rest on great precision. Of the two, Chekhov's dialogue is perhaps a trifle more colloquial than mine. Certainly in places it is more colloquial than I should ever dare to be; for in a translation any very marked colloquialism is always apt to hurt the economy of effect by raising questions as to what the original could have been to come out so patly as that.

Nevertheless, I can see how I might often give the impression of avoiding the literal or the Russian idiom. Indeed there are cases where the closer I stick to Chekhov the farther you may seem to think I am from him.

Suppose, for example, you have known the version of Trigorin's lines (ACT III) that says: "As if the field of art were not large enough to accommodate both old and new without the necessity of jostling," and chance now on my version: "There is room for all, the new and the old, why elbow?" You would be sure to think I had simplified the speech, otherwise what would account for the elaboration of the other, or even for turning the phrase *new and old* around? But what Chekhov says, exactly, is that there is room for all, the new and the old, why elbow?

You would think the same if you have known Trigorin's lines about the challenge as "—though what his provocation may be I can't imagine." Chekhov says, "But what for?"

Certainly I can remember myself accepting divers lines that only Chekhov's very text could have convinced me were not what he said.

For example, "I am irresistibly impelled toward her." Chekhov says, "I am drawn to her." And Chekhov says, "Every one writes as he wants to and as he can," but I used to think as a matter of course that it was what I had seen in a translation: "Every one writes in accordance with his desires and capacity."

By every reasonable argument, we should be able to say that detailed passages like the two following have been literally translated, whatever else they may be:

"A new novel of mine is nearing completion, and I still have to write an article for my complete works, which are about to appear."

"It was hard to find a taxidermist around this neighborhood. But it's real nice, isn't it?"

In Chekhov I find, however, that the first of these speeches reads:

"I'm in a hurry to finish a story, and, besides, I've promised to write something for an annual."

The second is not in Chekhov at all.

But before I know it, I will be giving the impression that the changes the translations may make in Chekhov's lines are all in the direction of the stuffy or elaborate or verbose, or—the reader, perhaps, may bring up the term —Mid-Victorian. Not at all. There are plenty of times when they take what is long and vivid, or vivid and short, and reduce it to what is short and flat. Here too the other translations may sound more faithful than mine. There are cases where I use words more concrete or lively than another translator uses, but he seems to be the one who follows the text exactly. The mere fact that he chooses the words he does, instead of indulging in others less general or colorless, would seem of itself to argue that.

"My play didn't strike your fancy," take that, for example, as I have written it. Its dramatic values are obvious, as coming from the poet, with his hurt pride, speaking to Nina, whom he loves. Versions like the Koteliansky and the Garnett "My play was not liked," and "You disliked my play," are so much flatter compared with it, that their only excuse would have to be their fidelity. They are not faithful, however. The common dictionary gives but one meaning for Chekhov's verb here: "To strike the fancy of."

There are plenty of these cases where the translator's flatness or colorlessness deceives you into thinking he strives to be literal. What goes on is about the same in them all—the Koteliansky's "I nearly fainted," or the Garnett's "It made me quite dizzy," for instance, where Chekhov has Arcadina say that everything is black before her eyes. Or take the Garnett's "It's beyond everything," or the Fell's "What the deuce does he mean by his impudence?" for Sorin's speech, instead of Chekhov's "The devil knows what it is."

As for the Mid-Victorian, that is a false scent. None of the seven translations of *The Sea Gull* is earlier than 1912, when the Calderon, the first and much the best, was published.

As for Russian sayings, idioms and so on, I am not the one avoiding them when the Garnett says, "You've got more money than you know what to do with." In Chekhov it is the popular saying about "more money than the chickens could pick up."

And I have to smile when I think of one of Trigorin's lines in ACT IV, and what tropes and idioms might seem to be abroad if I translated it just as Chekhov put it. Trigorin, describing his habits as an author, speaks of his reaction to a whiff of heliotrope:

(Fell): "I mutter to myself . . ."

(Koteliansky): "Immediately I register it in my mind . . ."

(Garnett): "I hurriedly make a note . . ."

The last two get the sense of it, but what Chekhov says is: "Quickly I wrap it around my mustache . . ."

This Russian saying, if I had used it, would have been about on the plane of our "comb that out of your whiskers" in the comic strips. Even at that I might have risked it but for the smell motif which the heliotrope suggests, and which would merely throw us off.

All translations of all texts must involuntarily break down at times, of course; we can only hope that no more than our share of such mistakes will befall us. Voluntary departures from Chekhov's text, however, are another matter entirely. In these the translator either tries to improve on the original, or, though he understands the words, does not see the point of what Chekhov is doing, and so takes matters into his own hands. In either case the result is the same, the change occurs. Meanwhile there are two things that any translation of *The Sea Gull* must try for. One is to write lines for Chekhov that are sayable on the stage; the other is to let Chekhov do things as he wants to do them.

Keeping Chekhov's lines sayable means putting them into a body of words and into a sentence-structure that could at least be spoken on the stage, and might at least be heard in ordinary conversation. The first is partly a physical matter, and depends to a great extent on the relation between the word-stresses and the sense-stresses, on whether or not the emphasis of the thought coincide with those of the words. The second is a concession to the demands of realism, or at any rate the demands of Chekhov's realistic method, and strives for speech that will sound natural and familiar.

Sayability has also, of course, its inner, or subjective

as it were, conditions. The readiness with which the actor can say a speech depends partly on what he feels about its relation to the character speaking and to the dramatic moment in which it belongs. He may glow with a sense of the perfect rightness, or very inspiration, of a speech he has to say. Or he may be checked by its inadequacy; or blocked by its falseness; or even embarrassed at the mere thought of having to say it at all. Imagine, for example, the actress whose Nina must, as in the Garnett, say to her adored author:

"You are overworked and have not the leisure nor the desire to appreciate your own significance."

Imagine the actor whose Trepleff, two lines before he goes out to kill himself, must say, as in the Koteliansky, "I have no faith, and don't know in what my vocation consists."

In one translation, Arcadina, enraged (ACT III), shrieks at her son, "Frump!" (a female term); in another, "Tatterdemalion!" (a literary one, which on the stage would sound like some foreign sentence).

Imagine the theatre ear that, however close the words may be to Dorn's speech about alcohol's effect on the ego, could write:

"Your 'I' dissolves in you, and you already take yourself for a third person—'he.'"

As for letting Chekhov do things as he wants to do them, there are plenty of cases where he has not been allowed that. One will serve—and a good, rank case of arbitrary change for no conceivable reason, it is. The words as Arcadina says them in Chekkhov are:

"Maupassant's *On the Water,*" and *"Pardon,* we are intruding."

The translations of Mrs. Garnett, for instance, Mr. Koteliansky, Mrs. Fell, Mr. Eisemann will not leave it so. They have:

"Sur l'eau," and *"Pardon . . ."*

" 'On the Water!' " . . . and, "I beg your pardon."

"Sur l'eau" . . . and, "Sorry to have disturbed you."

" 'On the Water' " . . . and "Kindly excuse our interruption."

There is another thing. In the theatre, time is as much of a reality as space is, perhaps more. To translate a speech, therefore, into one that changes its length to any noticeable extent is, quite apart from the words, to change also its meaning, exactly as might be true in a parallel sense of a sword, a kiss, a stair, a song. Take, for example, Shamreyeff's speech (ACT II) where he is shouting at Madame Arcadina: "You don't know what a farm means." In the Koteliansky it becomes: "You do not know what the management of an estate involves." In this case the difference in the meaning is as much a matter of the time-length as of the words, perhaps more so.

When it comes to patterns in structure, time is more important to the pattern *per se* than words are. Chekhov's patterns in *The Sea Gull* disappear either completely or partially—as a rule completely—in the translations; and where they do disappear, it is usually as much through changes in the time as changes in the words.

In ACT III, when Sorin has had a fainting attack and been urged to lie down, he has a little speech of two words and an *and*. It has both beginning rhyme and end rhyme, as anybody can see by the mere letters, whether he can read them or not—полежу и поеду. The device, as used here, is intended to suggest a stubborn whim and childishness.

The Garnett, the Koteliansky and the Fell lose both the pattern and the time-length when they say, respectively:

"I'll lie down a little and then set off."

"I'll lie down for a while and then go."

"I'll lie down a bit before I start."

My translation reads:

"I'm lying down and I'm going to town."

This at least retains the pattern. But since there is no

single word in English meaning to *lie down for a while*
and I had to add *to town* for the sake of the pattern, the
time-length in Chekhov's sentence is as lost to my translation as to the others. And this sort of difference, in
time, between a word in English and its equivalent in a
foreign language is something we cannot always hope
to manage. But the translator should at any rate be
aware that the problem exists.

Time-values are also related to the sense-stresses and
the directness of statement. For example, "What's left
is nothing," is only about six letters fewer than "There
is the merest trifle left," but the emphasis and the speak-
ability make it seem much briefer when spoken.

This time-element affects Chekhov's transitions. We
all know his method of combining details. Something is
said that apparently has no connection with what comes
before it or what seems to pop up after it; things seemingly unrelated are put next to each other; and lo, a
stream of life emerges from among them, a subcon-
scious unity, as it were. The very transitions themselves
are a part of what is expressed. The more complex, or
spread-out, or smudged, or unequally timed, these
different sections of a whole passage, the less easy the
transitions are likely to be, the less readily an underly-
ing unity will appear, the more confusing, arbitrary or
even grotesque the effect may seem. This will be found
to be the reason why in Mrs. Fell's translation particu-
larly some of Chekhov's transitions may seem to many
readers so unexpected, fantastic or even hilarious.

Mrs. Garnett's translation is the one most read and
most used in the theatre, and is both the best of all and
the worst. Violently wrong translation, which is to say,
a line that from the start is obviously off, can usually be
detected for what it is. The translation *per se* sticks out.
We see that something has happened and allow for that.
For example, Doctor Dorn could not be "humming" the
words "Tell her, my flowers . . ." Nor could Trepleff's
line about Trigorin be "marching like Hamlet and he

too with a book." Masha, when her foot is asleep, would not say, "I feel stiff in my leg"; nor would Nina emerge from behind the curtain with "Apparently, there's to be no continuation." Obviously Sorin would not say, "You've enjoyed yourself in your lifetime, but I?" Shamreyeff sighing for old times would not be "drawing his breath." And Nina, with the lake there at the back of the stage, could not say, "But this ocean attracts me with invisible power." Such passages as these scarcely involve the problem of translation; they can only, as Lucian would say, invite your incredulity.

But Mrs. Garnett's translation steals a march on us. It seems so sober, steady, painstaking and even, and conveys so unbroken an impression of scholarly care on the translator's part, that we could never think of it as anything but accurate. So that when it sounds mixed up, or intangible, or sometimes nearly incomprehensible, we assume that the fault must lie in Chekhov's text. He is evidently, we tell ourselves, that kind of author, marvelously intuitive at times and at times rather vague; and his translator is doing the best she can to give us an exact equivalent in English. We could not be worse mistaken.

With this in mind I have come back time and again to the Garnett translation of *The Sea Gull*. People are always telling me they saw this play some time or other, but did not know what it was about. Madame Ouspenskaya has said that she once tried to do Nina's last scene, using the Garnett; but found she could not act it, no matter how hard she tried, and in spite of her knowing the scene already in Russian. Even to memorize the lines seemed impossible. She tried then, out of that same volume, to do the governess in *The Cherry Orchard;* and though it was her own part, she could now do nothing with it. One of our most intelligent young American actors tells people that he played Trepleff sixty-three times in the Garnett version and still did not know what it was all about.

We may acknowledge our indebtedness to this translator and yet name her as the arch-contributor to that familiar conception of Chekhov as an author who is blurred, mystical, frustrated, et cetera. It is Mrs. Garnett most of all who will have to be disposed of before there can be any passable notion of what Chekhov is like.

The trouble is not only this scholar's lack of theatre knowledge. Throughout the whole translation there is a certain diffusion and a certain monotony of tone that is the very opposite of Chekhov's writing and that only her pages themselves could fully illustrate. Her style nearly always exhibits what is evidently her congenital lack of instinct for any and every sort of emphasis. (She is, for example, even in so simple a case, quite capable of, "What horses? How can I tell which", when there is Chekhov's, "What horses? How should I know—what horses!") She has a way of missing the point just enough to spoil the more immediate economy, as it were, of a theatre moment. In Trigorin's lines about heliotrope, for example, Mrs. Garnett speaks of "a sickly smell, a widow's flower," which only means that if we heard such a speech in the theatre, we should be stopping to wonder if the heliotrope's scent is really sickly, and if there is a flower for widowhood, or would that be something Russian? Which in turn would all be beside the point; what Chekhov says is "cloying smell, widow's color"; one of these is a matter of taste, and the other second mourning. Mrs. Garnett can go further and seriously miss the sense of Chekkhov's lines, though all the while she is turning out a grave and reassuring sentence that sounds like the restrained version of something that in the Russian original was gushing and incoherent. We shall see how it is precisely this that happens when she translates the schoolmaster's speech (ACT III) about Nina and Constantine and the play:

"They are in love with each other and today their souls will be united in the effort to realize the same artistic effect."

I stumbled on a rehearsal once just at a moment when the whole company had been brought to a halt by this

sentence. Nobody knew what it meant. But clearly it
meant nothing. Nearly all the important terms, such as
"in the effort," "realize," "same," "artistic," and "effect," have been translated wrong. "Be united" coming
after "in love with each other" has a distracting matri-
monial connotation. Otherwise "united" might do of
course; the gist of Chekhov's word is "to mingle," as of
two streams. "Realize" delays us by sounding as if it
were used exactly or significantly, whereas actually it
means nothing at all as used here. You can realize your
design in an artistic effect, or you can realize what an
artistic effect would be, and so on; but you cannot realize
an effect; the effect itself is the realization. Chekhov's
word means not to "realize," but to "give," to "bestow
on." "Artistic effect" is a hopelessly banal phrase, and
not the idea anyway. One of the Chekhov words can
mean either "artistic" or "art" as in "art theatre"; the
other means "image," not "effect"; the phrase means an
"art image" or "image in art." "In an effort" is not what
Chekhov says: "aspire" is the root-idea of the word he
uses. And "same" makes no sense. The same as what?
Chekhov says "one and the same." The schoolmaster's
idealistic theorizing colors this remark; he says—literally
—that today their souls are mingled in an aspiration to
give one and the same art image. "To give in [terms of]
art" might be more or less expressed by "create." The
feeling of "one and the same" is of "both in one and
one in both." Retaining its idealistic tint and remembering the theatre, we could say "today their souls are
mingled in a longing to create an image both can share
and true to both."

Sometimes this blur, or monotony, or whatever it is,
in Mrs. Garnett's lines is caused by her refusal to repeat
a word where Chekhov repeats it. How, then, is her
reader, or the audience that hear her version of *The
Sea Gull,* to guess from some plain sentence that Chekhov has a pattern here, neat or lyric or frankly
theatrical? Without the repetition, too, it may happen

that the reader misses the emphasis Chekhov intended. Or he may find the effect vague, weak, inconclusive and so on, without seeing that this happens because of the seemingly pointless synonyms that are used. Check through the play and you will note that Mrs. Garnett rarely allows Chekhov a repetition.

On the other hand, this same unwillingness to repeat the word creates sometimes a distinct effect of subtle values and analytical intentions that Chekhov never dreamt of. For example, when Constantine speaks of his mother as a famous actress and a few lines further on of his father as a well-known actor, one might think that Chekhov was making some distinction about mother and son and father, or art in the family. But he uses one word for both, to be translated "famous" or "well-known" as you choose, but not first one and then the other. When Trigorin, after a good deal of talk about life and about science, suddenly speaks of "life and culture," the implication is that the things he has been talking of must, when absorbed and animated by life, become culture. The discussion thus invited is a far cry from Chekhov's plain phrase "life and science," as two distinct fields of Trigorin's interest.

In this matter of the words especially, we need to let Chekhov do the thing as he wants to do it. Mr. John Anderson, in a recent article, made a searching comment (and here I am obliged to leave my own praises in or else disturb his point) on this subject:

"Doubtless," he says, "because he was a doctor Chekhov revealed a clinical detachment towards his characters as if concentrating on a group of symptoms. But if the method seems scientifically cold the manner has the warmth of a family physician—a man who would tell the truth, but gently. It is this family viewpoint in the plays, a sort of indulgent candor, which relieves these portraits of harshness and invests the Chekhov gallery with a tone of compassionate analysis.

"This sense of diagnosis, I think, stands the plays in

stead of the conventional plot. Chekhov's plotlessness
has become a commonplace of criticism and like many
critical clichés identifies something without bothering to
examine it. Plot or no plot, it is obvious that these plays
have a suspensive action that holds with the loose
strength of an open link chain. Their internal pattern
is bound to be a matter of words and half-suggested
meanings, and that is why this new version of *The Sea
Gull* is so important. For the first time the English-
speaking theatre has, in Mr. Young's retranslation, an
authoritative disclosure of Chekhov's true method. This
method is but vaguely realized in the previous translations, with their indifference, inexperience or ignorance,
when it came to the demands of stage speech. In all fair-
ness to Mrs. Garnett, however, as the best known of the
Chekhov translators, it may be pointed out that her con-
temporary English theatre offered no incentive to ex-
plore the verbal element which as we now see lies at the
core and holds the subtlest meaning of Chekhov's
dramas."

This is a fair comment, as coming from the theatre,
on Mrs. Garnett's lines; and it is only fair also to say
that on this theatre score she was really disinterested as
to what was right. The question remains, however, of
Chekhov and the words that, theatre or no theatre, he
chose to write in. Obviously Mrs. Garnett could claim
to be a Russian scholar, and obviously she could resort
like anybody else to a simple dictionary. We must conclude, then, that whatever she turns a Chekhov line into
is not what she may see it is but, if there is any question
in the matter, what she thinks it should be.

Take, for example, the passage where Trepleff and
his mother are in a crisis about Trigorin, and she has
just said she respects that man and must ask Trepleff
not to speak ill of him in her presence.

"TREPLEFF. And I don't respect him. You want
me to think him a genius, too; but forgive me, I can't
tell lies, his books make me sick.

"ARCADINA. That's envy. There's nothing left for people who have pretension without talent but to attack real talent. Much comfort in that, I must say!

"TREPLEFF (ironically). Real talent! (wrathfully) I have more talent than all of you. . . ."

It is not "books." The word means productions, compositions, creations, works, but only indirectly books. The difference here, for purposes of characterization and drama, is clear. As to, "'There's nothing left for people who have pretension without talent but to attack real talent," it has about all the troubles a sentence can be cursed with, especially for stage purposes. But we will let that pass and come to the sheer business of the words. It is not "without talent," Chekhov uses the adjective, "not talented," and leaves the one noun, which in turn is not "talent" but "talents" (Arcadina does not mean any abstraction, she means two people, herself and Trigorin, which is much better drama). And the dictionary defines the verb here, порицать, as to censure, disapprove, accuse, reproach, disparage, rather than to attack.

If we follow Chekhov as to verbs, adjectives, the order of the words, and so on, we find that the sentence goes thus: "For people not talented but pretentious of it, nothing else is left but to disparage real talents." Or, "People who are not talented but pretend to be have nothing better to do than to disparage real talents."

None of the other translators will allow Chekhov his own words for this passage. They say, "without talent, and with only pretensions"; "with no talent and with mighty pretensions"; and "more talented," "really gifted," "cleverer"; they say without exception, "real talent," never as in Chekhov, "real talents," and so on.

One of the most tender, searching and carefully built passages in *The Sea Gull,* and in all Chekhov, is that in the last act where Sorin speaks of what he has wanted in life and never had, and now will give to his nephew as the subject for a story. The seeming simplicity of this passage could scarcely carry more of the delicate and infallible devices that Chekhov openly employs for it.

In my translation *never* is used for the negative. It means here the same thing, and using it allows the verb to change its form, as it does in Chekhov—for example *marry, never married* instead of *marry, did not marry.*

"SORIN: Listen, I want to give Kostya a subject for a story. It should be called: 'The Man Who Wanted To—' *L'homme qui a voulu.* In my youth long ago wanted to become an author—and never became one; wanted to speak eloquently—and spoke execrably *(mimicking* himself) : 'and so on and so forth, and all the rest of it, yes and no' . . . and in the résumé would drag on, drag on, till the sweat broke out; wanted to marry—and never married; wanted always to live in town—and now am ending up my life in the country, and so on.

"DORN: Wanted to become a State Councillor—and became one.

"SORIN: (laughing) That I never longed for. That came of itself."

There are three effective devices used in this passage. One of these devices appears in the translations, sometimes more, sometimes less. It consists of the parallels in structure that are to be found in the four "wanted" sentences. The first and third of these sentences are shorter, with the latter half negative; the second and fourth are longer, with the latter half made up of contrasting words.

Of the two other devices, one consists of the parallels in words, not only the *wanted,* but also *become—became, speak—spoke, marry—married, always to live—ending up my life, become—became.* This device is partially observed in the divers translations.

The third has wholly disappeared from them all. It is the most subtle and most poignant of the three devices, and concerns the *wanted* and the pronouns *I* and *you.* (We must note here that pointing out this device does not mean that it would be incorrect to introduce the pronoun *I* into the Russian meanings. But Chekhov has so plainly been careful to keep this pronoun from sight, where in plenty of other places he uses it, that his intention is clear.) In this particular case Chekhov gets his effect by having, with one exception, no pronoun at all, neither *I* nor *he*, with *wanted*. By this means he throws the pathetic emphasis on that motif of long desiring. The exception is an *I* before the first *to become*, but not before the *wanted*. In English such an order for the words is impossible. We can keep the word-pattern, however, and the sense as well, by inserting the pronoun *my* before *youth*. With that one, half-hidden exception, then, in Chekhov's arrangement it is only at the very last that the first person pronoun appears, and then the *I* ripples out laughing in that little reply of Sorin's, scattering the pattern—the *wanted* has already disappeared. And in the meantime this *I* has already been prepared for by the *my* in Sorin's "ending up my life . . ."

(Koteliansky): *"The Man who wanted—L'Homme qui a vuolu.* In my young days long ago I wanted to become an author—and didn't; I always wanted to live in town . . . etc."

"DORN. You wanted to become a State Councillor—and became one.

"SORIN. That I didn't aspire to. . . . etc."

If the Koteliansky is to put those *I*'s into Sorin's first speech, then it is purely arbitrary to change to *you* when Dorn speaks. In Chekhov it is the same word, meaning "wanted," whether with an *I* or with a *he*. And putting the *always* before *wanted* instead of after it, not only changes the sense but still further spoils the pattern. Throughout the speech, in fact, this translation loses most of the word-parallels.

(Fell): " 'The Man Who Wished' . . . When I was young, I wished to be an author! I failed"—the clause *When I was* gets in the way of the *I wished*, not to mention those two *I*'s, plus the third *I* with *failed*, which

throws away Chekhov's parallel in *to become—never became*. The *long ago* is omitted. "I wished to be an orator; I speak abominably . . . etc."
"DORN. You wished, etc."

(Garnett) : " 'The Man Who Wished' . . . In my youth I wanted to become a literary man—and didn't; . . . I wanted to get married—and I didn't; . . . etc." Besides other defects, this translation does not even carry the title into the rest, what with *wished . . . wanted*.

(Editor, Rubin) : " 'The Man who wanted to' . . . When I was a young man I wanted to be a writer, and I didn't become one; . . . I wanted to marry and re-mained a bachelor . . . etc."

Nevertheless, it is remarkable how, in spite of these slights and losses from the translations, this passage of Chekhov's, not with all the fineness, and care, to be sure, and quivering sharp animation, not with all its elaborate half-covered contrivance, but with dramatic force, nevertheless, and telling stage effect, comes through.

You might think that if anything in *The Sea Gull* had a chance of coming through in translation as Chekhov planned it in Russian, Trigorin's speech (ACT II) about his success would be that thing. The progression of thought and feeling in this speech is so continuous, the single items so exact, and the integration—even that final sentence of eleven lines—so alive, that the attention of the audience finds it hard to stray. This is the way the speech goes in the Chekhov, keeping the order of words and even the punctuation :
"What success ? I have never pleased myself. I don't like myself as a writer. The worst of it is that I am in a sort of daze and often don't understand what I write— I love this water here, the trees, the sky, I feel nature, it stirs in me a passion, an irresistible desire to write. But

I am not only a landscape painter I am a citizen too, I love my country, the people, I feel that if I am a writer, I ought to speak also of the people, of their sufferings, of their future, speak of science, of the rights of man, and so on and so forth, and I speak of everything, I hurry up, on all sides they are after me, are annoyed at me, I dash from side to side like a fox baited by hounds, see life and science getting always farther and farther ahead as I fall always more and more behind, like a peasant missing his train, and the upshot is I feel that I can write only landscape, and in all the rest I am false and false to the marrow of my bones."

But for all his completeness of tone and mood, and all his articulation, Chekhov did not escape. I will quote Mrs. Fell's translation of that passage, putting in CAPITALS what is added to the Chekhov, and in *italics* what is left out.

"What success HAVE I HAD? I have never pleased myself; as a writer, I do not like myself AT ALL. The trouble is that I AM MADE GIDDY, AS IT WERE, BY THE FUMES OF MY BRAIN, and often HARD-LY know what I am writing. I love this lake, THESE trees, the BLUE heaven; NATURE'S VOICE SPEAKS TO ME AND wakes a FEELING OF passion in my HEART, AND I AM OVERCOME BY an uncontrollable desire to write. But I am not only a painter of landscapes, I am a MAN OF THE CITY besides. I love my country, TOO, AND her people; I feel that, AS a writer, it is my duty *also* to speak of *the people,* of their sorrows, of their future, ALSO *speak* of science, of the rights of man, and so forth. (STOP) So I WRITE on every subject, and THE PUBLIC hounds me on all sides. SOMETIMES in anger, and I race AND DODGE like a fox with A PACK of hounds on his trail. I see life and KNOWLEDGE FLITTING AWAY BEFORE ME. (STOP) I AM LEFT be-hind THEM like a peasant WHO HAS missed his train AT A STATION, and finally I come BACK to the conclusion that ALL I AM FIT FOR is to DESCRIBE landscapeS, and that WHATEVER ELSE I ATTEMPT RINGS ABOMINABLY FALSE."

Mrs. Garnett follows the speech closely, except for three unfortunate changes. Nature does not stir in Trigorin "a passion, an irresistible desire to write" but "a passionate, irresistible desire to write." He is not in a daze but in a "delirium," which is not what Chekhov says—the idiom в чаду, in a daze, is from чад, the word for kitchen smoke. And delirium does not describe this state of mind so familiar to creative people. She does not repeat "science," but changes "life and science" to "life and culture"; and the pattern of the thought in the speech is thus broken up. In the last line one "false" is omitted.

The Koteliansky breaks the word-pattern contrived in the whole speech by changing "write" landscape to "Compose." In the Eisemann translation the entire paragraph is reduced to these two lines: "Popularity? What popularity? I've never liked my own work. The author Trigorin doesn't appeal to me at all."

At the beginning of ACT III, we have the speech about the book inscriptions.

Masha has been telling Trigorin her plan to marry the schoolmaster and tear love out of her heart. A glass or so more and she regrets that Trigorin is leaving, she thanks him for his friendly interest, asks him to send her his books, and not to write in them "most esteemed lady," but simply this:

"To Maria, who not remembering her origin, does not know why she is living in this world."

The pitiful undercurrent is clear: she realizes that the decision to marry the man she does not love means the end of life for her; and in the release and insight, both confused and sharp, of alcohol, she is—consciously or sub-consciously—writing her own epitaph. Her speech is a parody of tombstone inscriptions.

A part of the genius of this scene consists in the way

in which it prevents us from settling on any one element in it, and from classifying the things it creates and the responses we feel. We are suspended here as life sometimes suspends us for the moment; and during that moment we fully sense our experience and are only vaguely conscious as yet of our decisions. And thus for a moment the mood is almost indistinguishable from life. The means by which, in the present scene, this whole effect is held together is partly wit, which in turn culminates in Chekhov's take-off of tombstone inscriptions. And this wit depends for its security on our recognition of the resemblance. The speech lives or dies, therefore, by its precision. In the form alone lie much of its meaning and all its point.

The *who*, in the Russian text, is implied. My translation is otherwise strictly literal, down, in fact, to the order of the words. We may note how the following translations vary in their relation to the Chekkhov, even with regard to the form of the girl's name.

(Koteliansky): "To Marie, a nobody, who's living in this world for no known reason."

(Garnett): "To Marya, who belongs nowhere and has no object in life."

(Fell): "To Masha, who, forgetful of her origin, for some unknown reason is living in this world."

(Editor, Rubin): "To Masha, 22, of no occupation, born into this world for no apparent purpose."

It is easy to see how a producer would be tempted to substitute other lines from Shakespeare for those Chekhov introduced into the scene (ACT I) between Arcadina and her son, just before his play begins. The scene is terrific enough without these lines to make it more so. Nevertheless, after reading the Garnett translation of *The Sea Gull* and after the productions I have seen on the stage, I was surprised to find what the Chekhov is. Trepleff begs his mother's patience, the play will soon begin, and she replies out of "Hamlet":

"My son!
Thou turnst mine eyes into my very soul,
And there I see such black and grained spots
As will not leave their tinct."

The Fell translation omitted Trepleff's reply entirely,
the Calderon gives the Shakespeare lines but recom-
mends substituting the lines that are now to be found
in the Garnett and in divers stage versions:
"Leave wringing of your hands, Peace, sit you down!
And let me wring your heart; for so I shall
If it be made of penetrable stuff."

These, of course, are lines from the earlier part of
the Closet Scene, transferred to follow here with a certain apropos and clever patness. But they are not in
character generally for Trepleff, they vulgarize his in-
tensity, and are out of key with his next reactions
towards his mother. Actually the reply that Chekhov has
written for Trepleff follows the lines in which Hamlet
replies to his mother in the Shakespeare scene:
"Nay, but to live
In the rank sweat of an enseamed bed,
Stew'd in corruption, honeying and making love
Over the nasty sty!"

These are appalling and obscene enough lines for
Hamlet to have to speak, even to an Elizabethan audience, with its stomach for audacities. A modern Trepleff
would find them impossible. Spoken thus at the beginning of the play, they would break up the company
gathered there in Sorin's park. On this basis some of
the translators and producers might seem to be right in
their substitutions or omissions. At any rate the Koteliansky translation is undoubtedly wrong to include as it
does the whole four lines from Shakespeare. In Chekhov's text these lines are not quoted. A paraphrase is
made of them, and a brief paraphrase at that:

"And why do you yield to sin, seek love in the depths of wickedness?"

And even with Hamlet's lines toned down like that, we have also the horn blowing for the play to begin, and are allowed a second only before the next impression. In such cases, nevertheless, it would seem to me advisable for the translator, if he does make so distinct a change or substitution, to see that the readers of Chekhov in English know of it.

I must thank Mrs. Catherine Alexander Burland for her contagious enthusiasm about a translation of a play and an author long beloved by her, and for the advice she gave when there was need of it. To show her a list of problems was to have it answered, both immediately and with remarkable literary tact where one language seemed to challenge the possibilities of another.

BIOGRAPHICAL NOTE

Anton Chekhov was born in Taganrog, Russia, on January 17, 1860. He was of peasant stock; the grandfather had bought the freedom of his family. At twenty Chekhov began writing, under the signature of Antosha Chekhonté. In 1884 he took his degree of Doctor of Medicine. In 1888 he was awarded the Pushkin prize of 500 rubles, by the Imperial Academy of Sciences. The mass of his writings grew steadily larger, but only the plays concern us here.

The Swan Song, a one-act play, was written in 1886; *Ivanoff*, a play in four acts, in 1887, produced in Moscow at Korsh's Theatre and in Petersburg. He wrote *The Wood Demon*, a comedy in four acts, and *A Tragedian Against His Will*, and *The Proposal*, farces, in 1889. By November, 1895, he had finished *The Sea Gull*, which was produced next year at the Alexandrinsky Theatre in Petersburg. It was a sorry failure. When produced by the Moscow Art Theatre the next year the play was a triumphant success.

Since we are especially engaged for the moment with *The Sea Gull*, it should be remarked here that both the early failure and the later success have been rather played up, as time went on, in a single, special light, not without an element of the theatre in it. At the Alexandrinsky, *The Sea Gull* was produced at a benefit performance for a popular comedienne, and the audience of her admirers scarcely expected, and was in no mood to enjoy, a play like this of Chekhov's. The response was appalling enough, but there were some who applauded the play; and in the course of the few repetitions, a certain amount of appreciation was shown, and friends made for the future. At the Moscow Art Theatre, on the other hand, there was a furor, and then a great ovation; but the house was half empty; and the excitement did not mean any great popular acceptance. None of Chekhov's plays won any real triumph until its second season; and even after that, it had to wait a long time before it drew large houses.

In 1889 *Uncle Vanya* was produced by the Moscow Art Theatre. *The Cherry Orchard* was finished in the autumn of 1903, and produced by the Moscow Art Theatre the following January. Chekhov died that same year, July 2, 1904, at Badenweiler, a German health resort, and was buried in Moscow.

TRANSLATIONS OF THE SEA GULL

The translations of *The Sea Gull* to which I have so
constantly referred are those by Julius West; George
Calderon; Marian Fell; Constance Garnett (in The
Modern Library, with an Introduction by Eva Le Galli-
enne, who with her Civic Repertory Theatre did more
about Chekhov in America than any one else has done);
S. S. Koteliansky (in Everyman's Library); and a
volume of Chekhov's plays published by the Arden
Book Company, in which "the publishers and editor are
indebted to Miss Rose N. Rubin for recommendations
concerning the selection and arrangement of The Plays
of Anton Chekhov." In magazine form, there is also the
translation by Fred Eisemann: Poet Lore, 1913.

THE SEA GULL

A COMEDY IN FOUR ACTS

CHARACTERS IN THE PLAY

(8 Males; 6 Females)

IRINA NICOLAYEVNA ARCADINA, MADAME TREPLEFF, *an actress*

CONSTANTINE GAVRILOVITCH TREPLEFF, *her son*

PETER NICOLAYEVITCH SORIN, *her brother*

NINA MIKHAILOVNA ZARYECHNY, *a young girl, the daughter of a wealthy landowner*

ILYA AFANASYEVITCH SHAMREYEFF, *a retired lieutenant, Sorin's steward*

PAULINE ANDREYEVNA, *his wife*

MASHA (MARYA ILYINISHNA), *his daughter*

BORIS ALEXEYEVITCH TRIGORIN, *a literary man*

EUGENE SERGEYEVITCH DORN, *a doctor*

SEMYON SEMYONOVITCH MEDVEDENKO, *a schoolmaster*

YACOV, *a laborer*

COOK

Two housemaids

THEATRE PROGRAM

The Alfred Lunt and Lynn Fontanne production of *The Sea Gull*, presented by The Theatre Guild, Inc., opened at the Shubert Theatre, March 28, 1938, with the following cast:

IRINA NICOLAYEVNA ARCADINA, MADAME TREPLEFF, *an actress* .... *Lynn Fontanne*

CONSTANTINE GAVRILOVITCH TREPLEFF, *her son*
—*Richard Whorf*

PETER NICOLAYEVITCH SORIN, *her brother, a retired Actual State Councillor, officially on a plane with Major-general or Rear-admiral* . *Sydney Greenstreet*

NINA MIKHAILOVNA ZARYECHNY, *a young girl, the daughter of a wealthy landowner* ...... *Uta Hagen*

ILYA AFANASYEVITCH SHAMREYEFF, *a retired lieutenant, Sorin's steward* .... *Harold Moffet*

PAULINE ANDREYEVNA, *his wife* .... *Edith King*

MASHA (MARYA ILYINISHNA), *his daughter*
—*Margaret Webster*

BORIS ALEXEYEVITCH TRIGORIN, *a literary man*
—*Alfred Lunt*

EUGENE SERGEYEVITCH DORN, *a doctor* . *John Barclay*

SEMYON SEMYONOVITCH MEDVEDENKO, *a schoolmaster*
—*O. Z. Whitehead*

YACOV, *a laborer* .... *Alan Hewitt*

COOK .... *S. Thomas Gomez*

HOUSEMAIDS ....⎰ *Jacqueline Paige*
⎱*Ernestine De Backer*

The action is laid at Sorin's country place. Between the Third and Fourth Acts two years elapse.

Translated by Stark Young
Directed by Robert Milton
Settings and costumes by Robert Edmond Jones

ACT ONE

A section of the park on SORIN'S *estate. The wide
avenue leading away from the spectators into the
depths of the park toward the lake is closed by a
platform hurriedly put together for private the-
atricals, so that the lake is not seen at all. To left
and right of the platform there are bushes. A few
chairs, a small table.*

*The sun has just set. On the platform behind the curtain
are* YACOV *and other workmen; sounds of cough-
ing and hammering are heard.* MASHA *and* MED-
VEDENKO *enter on the Left, returning from a walk.*

MEDVEDENKO. Why do you always wear black?
MASHA. I am in mourning for my life. I'm unhappy.
MEDVEDENKO. You unhappy? I can't understand it.
Your health is good, and your father is not rich but he's
well enough off. My life is much harder to bear than
yours. I get twenty-three roubles a month, and that's
all, and then out of that the pension fund has to be
deducted, but I don't wear mourning.

(They sit down.)

MASHA. It isn't a question of money. Even a beggar
can be happy.
MEDVEDENKO. Yes, theoretically he can, but not when
you come right down to it. Look at me, with my mother,
my two sisters and my little brother, and my salary
twenty-three roubles in all. Well, people have to eat and
drink, don't they? Have to have tea and sugar? Have
tobacco? So it just goes round and round.

3

MASHA. *(Glancing towards the stage)* The play will begin soon.

MEDVEDENKO. Yes. The acting will be done by Nina Zaretchny and the play was written by Constantine Gavrilovitch. They are in love with each other, and today their souls are mingled in a longing to create some image both can share and true to both. But my soul and your soul can't find any ground to meet on. You see how it is. I love you; I can't stay at home because I keep wishing so for you; and so every day I walk four miles here and four miles back and meet with nothing but indifference on your side. That's only natural. I've got nothing, we're a big family. Who wants to marry a man who can't even feed himself?

MASHA. Fiddlesticks! *(She takes snuff)* Your love touches me, but I can't return it, that's all. *(Offers him snuff)* Help yourself.

MEDVEDENKO. I'd as soon not.

(A pause.)

MASHA. My, how close it is! It must be going to storm tonight. All you do is philosophise or talk about money. You think the worst misery we can have is poverty. But I think it's a thousand times easier to go ragged and beg for bread than— But you'd never understand that—

(Enter SORIN, leaning on his walking stick, and TREPLEFF.)

SORIN. For some reason, who knows, my dear boy, the country's not my style. Naturally. You can't teach an old horse new tricks. Last night I went to bed at ten o'clock, and at nine this morning I awoke feeling as if my brain stuck to my skull, and so on. *(Laughing)* And then on top of all that I fell asleep after dinner just the same. And so now I'm a wreck, I'm still lost in a nightmare, and all the rest of it.

TREPLEFF. That's true, Uncle, you really ought to live in town. *(Sees* MASHA *and* MEDVEDENKO) Look, my friends, we'll call you when the play starts, but don't stay here now. I'll have to ask you to go.

SORIN. *(To* MASHA) Maria Ilyinishna, won't you kindly ask your father to leave that dog unchained, to stop that howling? All last night again my sister couldn't sleep.

MASHA. You'll have to tell my father yourself. I shan't do it, so please don't ask me to. *(To* MEDVEDENKO) Let's go.

MEDVEDENKO. Then you'll let us know before the play starts.

(MASHA *and* MEDVEDENKO *go out.)*

SORIN. That just means the dog will howl all night again. You see how 'tis; in the country I have never had what I wanted. It used to be I'd get leave for twenty-eight days, say, and come down here to recoup, and so on; but they plagued me so with one silly piece of nonsense after another that the very first day I wanted to be out of it. *(Laughs)* I've always left here with relish. Well, now that I'm retired, I have nowhere to go and all the rest of it. Like it—like it not, I live—

YAKOV. We're going for a swim, Constantine Gavrilovitch.

TREPLEFF. So long as you are back in ten minutes. *(Looks at his watch)* We're about to begin.

YAKOV. Yes, sir.

TREPLEFF. Here's your theatre. The curtain, then the first wing, then the second wing, and still farther open space. No scenery at all. You see what the background is —it stretches to the lake and on to the horizon. And the curtain will go up at 8:30, just when the moon's rising.

SORIN. Magnificent!

TREPLEFF. If Nina's late, then, of course, the whole effect will be spoilt. It's time she were here now. But her father and stepmother watch her so she can hardly get out of the house, it's like escaping from prison. *(Straightening his uncle's tie)* Uncle, your hair and beard are rumpled up—oughtn't you to have them trimmed?

SORIN. *(Combing his beard)* It's the tragedy of my life. I always look as if I'd been drunk, even when I was young I did—and so on. Women never have loved me. *(Sits down)* Why is my sister in such bad humour?

TREPLEFF. Why? Bored. *(Sits down by SORIN)* Jealous. She's set against me, against the performance and against my play, because Nina's going to act in it and she's not. She's never read my play but she hates it.

SORIN. You *(Laughing)* imagine things, really.

TREPLEFF. Yes, she's furious because even on this little stage it's Nina will have a success and not she. *(Looks at his watch)* A psychological case, my mother: She's undeniably talented, intelligent, capable of sobbing over a novel; she recites all of Nekrassov's poetry by heart; she nurses the sick like an angel; but you just try praising Duse to her; Oh, ho! You praise nobody but her, write about her, rave about her, go into ecstasies over her marvelous performance in "La Dame Aux Camélias" or in "The Fumes of Life." But all that is a drug she can't get in the country, so she's bored and cross. We are all her enemies—it's all our fault. And then she's superstitious—afraid of three candles or number thirteen. She's stingy. She's got seventy thousand roubles in an Odessa bank, I know that for a fact. But ask her for a loan, she'll burst into tears.

SORIN. You've got it into your head your play annoys your mother, and that upsets you, and so forth. Don't worry, your mother worships the ground you walk on.

TREPLEFF. *(Picking petals from a flower)* Loves me —loves me not, loves me—loves me not, loves me— loves me not. *(Laughing)* You see, my mother doesn't love me, of course not. I should say not! What she wants is to live, and love, and wear pretty clothes; and here I am twenty-five years old and a perpetual reminder that she's no longer young. You see when I'm not there she's

only thirty-two, and when I am she's forty-three—and
for that she hates me. She knows too that I refuse to
admit the theatre. She loves the theatre; it seems to her
that she's working for humanity, for holy art. But to
my thinking her theatre today is nothing but routine,
convention. When the curtain goes up, and by artificial
light in a room with three walls, these great geniuses,
these priests of holy art, show how people eat, drink,
make love, move about and wear their jackets; when
they try to fish a moral out of these flat pictures and
phrases, some sweet little bit anybody could understand
and any fool take home; when in a thousand different
dishes they serve me the same thing over and over, over
and over, over and over—well, it's then I run and run
like Maupassant from the Eiffel Tower and all that vul-
garity about to bury him.

Sorin. But we can't do without the theatre.

Trepleff. We must have new forms. New forms we
must have, and if we can't get them we'd better have
nothing at all. *(He looks at his watch)* I love my mother
—I love her very much—but she leads a senseless life,
always making a fuss over this novelist, her name forever chucked about in the papers—it disgusts me. It's
just the simple egotism of an ordinary mortal, I suppose,
stirring me up sometimes that makes me wish I had
somebody besides a famous actress for a mother, and
fancy if she had been an ordinary woman I'd have
been happier. Uncle, can you imagine anything more
hopeless than my position is in her house? It used to be
she'd entertain, all famous people—actors and authors
—and among them all I was the only one who was nothing, and they put up with me only because I was her son.
Who am I? What am I? I left the university in my third
year, owing to circumstances, as they say, for which the
editors are not responsible; I've no talent at all, not a
kopeck on me; and according to my passport I am—a
burgher of Kiev. My father, as you know, was a
burgher of Kiev, though he was also a famous actor. So
when these actors and writers of hers bestowed on me

their gracious attentions, it seemed to me their eyes were measuring my insignificance. I guessed their thoughts and felt humiliated.

SORIN. By the by, listen, can you please tell me what sort of man this novelist is. You see I can't make him out. He never opens his mouth.

TREPLEFF. He's an intelligent man, he's simple, apt to be melancholy. Quite decent. He's well under forty yet but he's already celebrated, he's had more than enough of everything. As for his writings—well, we'll say charming, full of talent, but after Tolstoy or Zola, of course, a little of Trigorin goes a long way.

SORIN. My boy, I'm fond of writers, you know. Once there were two things I wanted passionately. To marry and to be an author. I never succeeded in doing either. It must be pleasant being a minor writer even, and all the rest of it.

TREPLEFF. I hear footsteps. *(Embraces his uncle)* I can't live without her. Just the sound of her footsteps is lovely. *(Going to meet* NINA ZARETCHNY *as she enters)* I'm insanely happy! My enchantress! My dream!

NINA. I'm not late, surely I'm not late.

TREPLEFF. *(Kissing her hands)* No, no, no.

NINA. All day I worried, was so frightened—I was so afraid father wouldn't let me come. But at last he's gone out. He went out just now with my stepmother. The sky has turned red, the moon will soon be up, and I raced the horse, raced him. *(Laughs)* But I'm so happy. *(Warmly shaking* SORIN's *hand.)*

SORIN. *(Laughing)* You've been crying, I see by your little eyes. That's not fair.

NINA. That's so. You can see how out of breath I am. Do let's hurry. I've got to go in half an hour. I must. Don't ask me to stay, my father doesn't know I'm here.

TREPLEFF. It's time to begin anyhow—I'll go call them.

SORIN. I'll go. I'll go this minute. *(Begins to sing "THE TWO GRENADIERS," then stops)* Once I started singing like that and a deputy who was standing

by said, "Your Excellency has a very strong voice"—
then he thought awhile and said, "Strong but unpleasant." *(Exits, laughing.)*

NINA. My father and his wife won't let me come
here; they say it's Bohemia. They are fraid I'll go on the
stage. But I am drawn here to this lake like a sea gull.
My heart is full of you.

TREPLEFF. We're alone.

NINA. Isn't that some one over there?

TREPLEFF. No, nobody. *(Kisses her.)*

NINA. What kind of tree is that?

TREPLEFF. It's an elm.

NINA. Why does it look so dark?

TREPLEFF. Because it's evening and everything looks
darker. Don't go away early, please don't.

NINA. I must.

TREPLEFF. But if I should follow you, Nina? I'll stand
all night in the garden, looking up at your window.

NINA. Oh, no! You mustn't. The watchman would
see you and Treasure doesn't know you yet, he'd bark.

TREPLEFF. I love you.

NINA. Ssh—!

TREPLEFF. Who's that?—You, Yakov?

YAKOV. *(From behind stage)* Yes, sir.

TREPLEFF. You must get to your seats, it's time to
begin. The moon's coming up.

YAKOV. Yes, sir.

TREPLEFF. Have you got that methylated spirit? Is
the sulphur ready? *(To NINA)* You see when the red
eyes appear there must be a smell of sulphur around.
You'd better go now, everything's ready. Do you feel
nervous?

NINA. Yes, awfully. It's not that I'm afraid of your
mother so much, it's Boris Trigorin terrifies me, acting
before him, a famous author like him. Tell me, is he
young?

TREPLEFF. Yes.

NINA. What marvelous stories he writes!

TREPLEFF. *(Coldly)* I don't know. I don't read them.

NINA. It's hard to act in your play. There are no living characters in it.

TREPLEFF. Living characters! I must represent life not as it is and not as it should be, but as it appears in my dreams.

NINA. In your play there's no action; it's all recitation. It seems to me a play must have some love in it.

(They go out by way of the stage. Enter PAULINE ANDREYEVNA *and* DORN.)

PAULINE. It's getting damp, go back and put on your galoshes.

DORN. I'm hot.

PAULINE. You don't take any care of yourself and it's just contrariness. You're a doctor and know very well how bad damp air is for you, but you like to make me miserable. You sat out on that terrace all last evening on purpose.

DORN. *(Sings low)* Oh, never say that I—

PAULINE. You were so enchanted by Madame Arcadina's conversation you didn't even notice the cold. You may as well own up—she charms you.

DORN. I'm fifty-five.

PAULINE. Fiddlesticks! What's that for a man, it's not old. You're still young enough looking—women still like you.

DORN. *(Gently)* Tell me, what is it you want?

PAULINE. Before an actress you are all ready to kiss the ground. All of you!

DORN. *(Sings low)* Once more I stand before thee— If society does make a fuss over actors, treats them differently from, say shopkeepers—it's only right and natural. That's the pursuit of the ideal.

PAULINE. Women have always fallen in love with you and hung on your neck. Is that the pursuit of the ideal too?

DORN. *(Shrugs his shoulders)* Why? In the relations women have had with me there has been a great deal that was fine. What they chiefly loved in me was the fact that I was a first-class doctor for childbirths. Ten or fifteen years ago, you remember, I was the only decent accoucheur they had in all this part of the country. Besides, I've always been an honorable man.

PAULINE. *(Clasping his hand)* My dear!

DORN. Ssh—here they come!

(Enter MADAME ARCADINA *on* SORIN'S *arm,* TRIGORIN, SHAMREYEFF, MEDVEDENKO, *and* MASHA.)

SHAMREYEFF. In '73 at the Poltava Fair—pure delight—I can assure you she was magnificent, ah, magnificent! Pure delight! But tell me if you know where Chadin, Paul Semyonovitch, the comedian, is now? Take his Raspluyef—'twas better than Sadovsky's, I can assure you, most esteemed lady. But what's become of him?

ARCADINA. You keep asking me about someone before the flood—how should I know? *(Sits down.)*

SHAMREYEFF. Ah *(Sighs)* Paulie Chadin! Nobody like that now. The stage is not what it was, Irina Nikolayevna, ah no! In those days there were mighty oaks, now we have nothing but stumps.

DORN. There are not many brilliant talents nowadays, it's true, but the general average of the acting is much higher.

SHAMREYEFF. I can't agree with you there. However, that's a matter of taste, *De gustibus aut bene, aut nihil.*

*(*TREPLEFF *comes out from behind the stage.)*

ARCADINA. My dear son, when does it begin?

TREPLEFF. Please be patient. It's only a moment.

ARCADINA. *(Reciting from* Hamlet) My son!
"Thou turnst mine eyes into my very soul,
  And there I see such black and grained spots
  As will not leave their tint."

TREPLEFF. *(Paraphrasing from* Hamlet) Nay, but to

live in wickedness, seek love in the depths of sin— *(Behind the stage a horn blows.)* Ladies and gentlemen, we begin! I beg your attention. *(A pause.)* I begin. *(Tapping the floor with a stick. In a loud voice)* Harken ye mists, out of ancient time, that drift by night over the bosom of this lake, darken our eyes with sleep and in our dream show us what will be in 200,000 years.

SORIN. In 200,000 years nothing will be.

TREPLEFF. Then let them present to us that nothing.

ARCADINA. Let them. We are asleep.

(The curtain rises. Vista opens across the lake. Low on the horizon the moon hangs, reflected in the water. NINA ZARETCHNY all in white, seated on a rock.)

NINA. Men and beasts, lions, eagles and partridges, antlered deer, mute fishes dwelling in the water, starfish and small creatures invisible to the eye—these and all life have run their sad course and are no more. Thousands of creatures have come and gone since there was life on the earth. Vainly now the pallid moon doth light her lamp. In the meadows the cranes wake and cry no longer; and the beetles' hum is silent in the linden groves. Cold, cold, cold. Empty, empty, empty! Terrible, terrible, terrible. *(A pause.)* Living bodies have crumbled to dust, and Eternal Matter has changed them into stones and water and clouds and there is one soul of many souls. I am that soul of the world.—In me the soul of Alexander the Great, of Cæsar, of Shakespeare, of Napoleon and of the lowest worm. The mind of man and the brute's instinct mingle in me. I remember all, all, and in me lives each several life again.

(The will-o'-the-wisps appear.)

ARCADINA. *(In a stage whisper)* We're in for something decadent.

TREPLEFF. *(Imploring and reproaching)* Mother!

NINA. I am alone. Once in a hundred years I open my lips to speak, and in this void my sad echo is unheard. And you, pale fires, you do not hear me. . . . Before daybreak the putrid marsh begets you, and you wander until sunrise, but without thought, without will, without the throb of life. For fear life should spring in you the father of eternal matter, the Devil, causes every instant in you, as in stones and in water, an interchange of the atoms, and you are changing endlessly. I, only, the world's soul, remain unchanged and am eternal. *(A pause)* I am like a prisoner cast into a deep, empty well, and know not where I am nor what awaits me. One thing only is not hidden from me: in the stubborn, savage fight with the devil, the principle of material forces, I am destined to conquer; and when that has been, matter and spirit shall be made one in the shadow of my soul forever. And lo, the kingdom of universal will is at hand. But that cannot be before long centuries of the moon, the shining dog star, and the earth, have run to dust. And till that time horror shall be, horror, horror, horror? *(A pause; upon the background of the lake appear two red spots.)* Behold, my mighty adversary, the Devil, approaches. I see his awful, blood-red eyes.

ARCADINA. I smell sulphur, is that necessary?

TREPLEFF. Yes, it is.

ARCADINA. Oh, I see *(Laughing)*—it's a stage effect!

TREPLEFF. Mother!

NINA. But without man he is lost—

PAULINE. *(To* DORN) You're taking your hat off. Put it on, you'll catch cold.

ARCADINA. The doctor has taken off his hat to the Devil, the father of Eternal Matter?

TREPLEFF. *(Blazing up, in a loud voice)* The play's over! That's enough! Curtain!

ARCADINA. Why are you angry?

TREPLEFF. That's enough. Curtain! Drop the curtain! *(Stamping his foot)* Curtain! *(The curtain falls.)* You must excuse me! I don't know how it was but I forgot somehow that only a chosen few can write plays and act them. I was infringing on a monopoly— My—I— *(Instead of saying more he makes a gesture of having done with it and goes out to the Left.)*

ARCADINA. What's the matter with him?

SORIN. Irina, my dear, you mustn't treat a young man's pride like that.

ARCADINA. Now what have I said?

SORIN. You've hurt his feelings.

ARCADINA. But he told us beforehand it was all in fun, that's the way I took it—of course.

SORIN. Just the same—

ARCADINA. And now it appears he's produced a masterpiece. Well, I declare! Evidently he had no intention of amusing us, not at all; he got up this performance and fumigated us with sulphur to demonstrate to us how plays should be written and what's worth acting in. I'm sick of him. Nobody could stand his everlasting digs and outbursts. He's an unruly, conceited boy.

SORIN. He was only hoping to give you some pleasure.

ARCADINA. Yes? I notice he didn't choose some familiar sort of play, but forced his own decadent raving on us. I can listen to raving. I don't mind listening to it, so long as I'm not asked to take it seriously; but this of his is not like that. Not at all, it's introducing us to a new epoch in art, inaugurating a new era in art. But to my mind it's not new forms or epochs, it's simply bad temper.

TRIGORIN. Every one writes as he wants to and as he can.

ARCADINA. Well, let him write as he wants to and as he can, so long as he leaves me out of it.

DORN. Great Jove angry is no longer Jove.

ARCADINA. I'm not Jove, I'm a woman. *(Lighting a cigarette)* I'm not angry—I'm merely vexed to see a young man wasting his time so. I didn't mean to hurt him.

MEDVEDENKO. Nobody has any grounds for separating matter from spirit, for it may be this very spirit itself is a union of material atoms. *(Excitedly, to TRIG-*

ORIN) You know, somebody ought to put in a play, and then act on the stage, how we poor schoolmasters live. It's a hard, hard life.

ARCADINA. That's so, but we shan't talk of plays or atoms. The evening is so lovely. Listen—they're singing! *(Pausing to listen)* How good it is!

PAULINE. It's on the other side of the lake.

(A pause.)

ARCADINA. Sit down by me here. *(To TRIGORIN)* You know, ten or fifteen years ago we had music on this lake every night almost. There were six big country houses then around the shore; and it was all laughter, noise, shooting and lovemaking—making love without end. The *jeune premier* and the idol of all six houses was our friend here, I must present *(Nods toward DORN)* Doctor Eugene Sergeyevitch. He's charming now, but then he was irresistible. Why did I hurt my poor boy's feelings? I'm worried about him. *(Calls)* Kostya! Son! Kostya!

MASHA. I'll go look for him.

ARCADINA. Would you, my dear?

MASHA. *(Calling)* Ah-oo! Constantine. Ah-oo! *(She goes out.)*

NINA. *(Coming from behind the stage)* Evidently we're not going on, so I may as well come out. Good evening! *(Kisses MADAME ARCADINA and PAULINE ANDREYEVNA.)*

SORIN. Bravo! Bravo!

ARCADINA. Bravo! Bravo! We were all enchanted. With such looks and such a lovely voice, it's a sin for you to stay here in the country. You have talent indeed. Do you hear? You owe it to yourself to go on the stage.

NINA. Oh, that's my dream. *(Sighing)* But it will never come true.

ARCADINA. Who can tell? Let me present Boris Alexeyevitch Trigorin.

NINA. Oh, I'm so glad— *(Much embarrassed)* I'm always reading your—

ARCADINA. *(Drawing* NINA *down beside her)* Don't be shy, dear. He may be a famous author, but his heart's quite simple. Look, he's embarrassed too.

DORN. I suppose we may raise the curtain now. This way it's frightening.

SHAMREYEFF. *(Loudly)* Yakov, my man, raise the curtain!

(The curtain is raised.)

NINA. *(To* TRIGORIN) It's a strange play, isn't it?

TRIGORIN. I didn't understand a word of it. However, I enjoyed watching it. You acted with so much sincerity, and the scenery was so lovely. *(A pause)* I dare say there are quantities of fish in this lake.

NINA. Yes.

TRIGORIN. I love fishing. I can think of no greater pleasure than to sit along towards evening by the water and watch a float.

NINA. But, I'd have thought that for any one who had tasted the joy of creation, no other pleasures could exist.

ARCADINA. *(Laughing)* Don't talk like that. When people make him pretty speeches he simply crumples up.

SHAMREYEFF. I remember one evening at the Opera in Moscow when the celebrated Silva was singing, how delighted we were when he took low C. Imagine our surprise—it so happened the bass from our church choir was there and all at once we heard "Bravo Silva" from the gallery a whole octave lower—like this—"Bravo Silva." The audience was thunderstruck.

(A pause.)

DORN. The angel of silence is flying over us.

NINA. Oh, I must go. Goodbye.

ARCADINA. Where to? Where so early? We won't allow it.

NINA. Papa is waiting for me.

ARCADINA. What a man, really! *(Kissing her)* Well, there's no help for it. It's too sad losing you.

NINA. If you only knew how I don't want to go.

ARCADINA. Somebody must see you home, child.

NINA. *(Frightened)* Oh, no, no.

SORIN. *(Imploring her)* Don't go.

NINA. I must, Peter Nicolayevitch.

SORIN. Stay an hour more, and so on. Come now, really!

NINA. *(Hesitating with tears in her eyes)* I can't. *(She shakes hands and hurries out.)*

ARCADINA. Now there's a really poor, unfortunate girl. They say her mother when she died willed the husband all her immense fortune, everything to the very last kopeck, and now this little girl is left with nothing, since her father has already willed everything he has to the second wife. That's shocking.

DORN. Yes, her papa is rather a beast, I must grant him that.

SORIN. *(Rubbing his hands to warm them)* What do you say, we'd better go in too, it's getting damp. My legs ache.

ARCADINA. It's like having wooden legs, you can hardly walk on them. Come on, you poor old patriarch. *(She takes his arm.)*

SHAMREYEFF. *(Offering his arm to his wife)* Madame?

SORIN. There's that dog howling again. *(To* SHAMREYEFF*)* Be good enough, Ilya Afanasyevitch, to tell them to let that dog off the chain.

SHAMREYEFF. It can't be done, Peter Nikolayevitch, or we'll be having thieves in the barn, and the millet's there. *(To* MEDVEDENKO *walking beside him)* Yes, a whole octave lower "Bravo Silva"! And not your concert singer, mind you, just ordinary church choir.

MEDVEDENKO. And what salary does a church singer get?

*(*ALL *except* DORN *go out.)*

DORN. *(Alone)* I don't know—maybe I'm no judge, I may be going off my head, but I liked that play. There's something in it. When the girl spoke of the vast solitude, and afterward when the Devil's eyes appeared, I could feel my hands trembling. It was all so fresh and naïve. But here he comes. I want to say all the nice things I can to him.

(Enter TREPLEFF.)

TREPLEFF. They've all gone.

DORN. I'm here.

TREPLEFF. Masha's been hunting for me all over the park. Unbearable creature!

DORN. Constantine Gavrilovitch, I admired your play extremely. It's a curious kind of thing and I haven't heard the end, but still it made a deep impression on me. You've got great talent. You must keep on! (CONSTANTINE *presses his hand and embraces him impulsively)* Phew, what a nervous fellow! Tears in his eyes! What I wanted to say is you chose your subject from the realm of abstract ideas, and that's right—a work of art should express a great idea. There is no beauty without seriousness. My, you are pale!

TREPLEFF. So you think—I ought to go on?

DORN. Yes. But write only of what is profound and eternal. You know how I have lived my life, I have lived it with variety and choiceness; and I have enjoyed it; and I am content. But if ever I had felt the elevation of spirit that comes to artists in their creative moments I believe I should have despised this body and all its usages, and tried to soar above all earthly things.

TREPLEFF. Forgive me, where's Nina?

DORN. And another thing. In a work of art there must be a clear, definite idea. You must know what your object is in writing, for if you follow that picturesque road without a definite aim, you will go astray and your talent will be your ruin.

TREPLEFF. *(Impatiently)* Where is Nina?

DORN. She's gone home.

TREPLEFF. *(In despair)* What shall I do? I want to see her. I must see her. I'm going—

(MASHA *enters.*)

DORN. Calm yourself, my friend!

TREPLEFF. But all the same I'm going. I must go.

MASHA. Constantine Gavrilovitch, come indoors. Your mother wants you. She's anxious.

TREPLEFF. Tell her I've gone—and please—all of you let me alone! Don't follow me around.

DORN. Come, come, come, boy, you mustn't act like this—it won't do.

TREPLEFF. *(In tears)* Goodbye, Doctor—and thank you— *(Exits.)*

DORN. *(Sighing)* Ah, youth, youth—

MASHA. When there is nothing else left to say, people always say, "Ah, youth, youth." *(Takes a pinch of snuff.)*

DORN. *(Takes snuff-box out of her hand and flings it into the bushes)* It's disgusting. *(A pause.)* There in the house they seem to be playing. We'd better go in.

MASHA. No, no, wait a minute.

DORN. What is it?

MASHA. Let me talk to you—I don't love my father, I can't talk to him, but I feel with all my heart that you are near me— Help me—help me— *(Starts to sob)* or I shall do something silly, I'll make my life a mockery, ruin it—I can't keep on—

DORN. How? Help you how?

MASHA. I'm tortured. No one, no one knows what I'm suffering— *(Laying her head on his breast, softly)* I love Constantine.

DORN. How nervous they all are! How nervous they all are! And so much love! O magic lake! *(Tenderly)* What can I do for you, child? What, what?

END OF ACT ONE

ACT TWO

A croquet lawn. In the background on the Right is the
house with a large terrace; on the Left is seen the
lake, in which the blazing sun is reflected. Flower-
beds. Noon. Hot. On one side of the croquet lawn,
in the shade of an old linden tree, MADAME ARCA-
DINA. DORN *and* MASHA *are sitting on a garden*
bench. DORN *has an open book on his knees.*

ARCADINA. *(To* MASHA) Here, let's stand up. *(They*
BOTH *stand up.)* Side by side. You are twenty-two and
I am nearly twice that. Doctor Dorn, tell us, which one
of us looks the younger?

DORN. You, of course.

ARCADINA. There you are—you see?—And why is it?
Because I work, I feel, I'm always on the go, but you sit
in the same spot all the time, you're not living. I make it
a rule never to look ahead into the future. I let myself
think neither of old age nor of death. What will be will
be.

MASHA. But I feel as if I were a thousand, I trail my
life along after me like an endless train.—Often I have
no wish to be living at all. *(Sits down)* Of course that's
all nonsense. I ought to shake myself and throw it all off.

DORN. *(Sings softly)* Tell her, pretty flowers—

ARCADINA. Then I'm correct as an Englishman. I'm
always dressed and my hair always *comme il faut.* Would
I permit myself to leave the house, even to come out here
in the garden, in a dressing-gown or with my hair
blousy? Never, I should say not! The reason I have
kept my looks is because I've never been a frump, never
let myself go, as some do. *(Arms akimbo, she walks up*
and down the croquet green) Here I am, light as a bird.
Ready to play a girl of fifteen any day.

20

DORN. Well, at any rate, I'll go on with my reading. *(Takes up the book)* We stopped at the corn merchants and the rats.

ARCADINA. And the rats. Go on. *(Sits)* Let me have it, I'll read. It's my turn anyhow. *(She takes the book and looks for the place)* And the rats—here we are— *(Reads)* "And certainly, for people of the world to pamper the romantics and make them at home in their houses is as dangerous as for corn merchants to raise rats in their granaries. And yet they are beloved. And so when a woman has picked out the author she wants to entrap, she besieges him with compliments, amenities and favors." Well, among the French that may be, but certainly here with us there's nothing of the kind, we've no set program. Here with us a woman before she ever sets out to capture an author is usually head over heels in love with him herself. To go no further, take me and Trigorin—

(Enter SORIN, leaning on a stick, with NINA at his side. MEDVEDENKO follows him, pushing a wheel chair.)

SORIN. *(Caressingly, as if to a child)* Yes? We're all joy, eh? We're happy today after all. *(To his sister)* We're all joy. Father and stepmother are gone to Tver, and we are free now for three whole days.

NINA. *(Sits down beside ARCADINA and embraces her)* I am so happy! I belong now to you.

SORIN. *(Sitting down in the wheel chair)* She looks lovely today.

ARCADINA. Beautifully dressed, intriguing—that's a clever girl. *(She kisses NINA)* We mustn't praise her too much. It's bad luck. Where's Boris Alexeyivitch?

NINA. He's at the bath-house fishing.

ARCADINA. You'd think he'd be sick of it. *(She begins reading again.)*

NINA. What is that you have?

ARCADINA. Maupassant's "On The Water," darling. *(Reads a few lines to herself)* Well, the rest is uninteresting and untrue. *(Shutting the book)* I'm troubled in my soul. Tell me, what's the matter with my son? Why is he so sad and morose. He spends day after day on the lake and I hardly ever see him any more.

MASHA. His heart's troubled. *(To* NINA, *timidly)* Please, Nina, read something out of his play, won't you?

NINA. *(Shrugging her shoulders)* You really want me to? It's so uninteresting.

MASHA. *(With restrained eagerness)* When he recites anything his eyes shine and his face grows pale. He has a beautiful sad voice, and a manner like a poet's.

(Sound of SORIN'S *snoring.)*

DORN. Pleasant dreams.
ARCADINA. *(To* SORIN) Petrusha!
SORIN. Eh?
ARCADINA. Are you asleep?
SORIN. Not at all.

(A pause.)

ARCADINA. You are not following any treatment for yourself, that's not right, brother.

SORIN. I'd be glad to follow a treatment, but the doctor won't give me any.

DORN. Take care of yourself at sixty!

SORIN. Even at sixty a man wants to live.

DORN. *(Impatiently)* Bah! Take your valerian drops.

ARCADINA. I'd think it would do him good to take a cure at some springs.

DORN. Well—he might take it. He might not take it.

ARCADINA. Try and understand that!

DORN. Nothing to understand. It's all clear.

(A pause.)

MEDVEDENKO. Peter Nikolayevitch ought to give up smoking.

SORIN. Fiddlesticks!

DORN. No, it's not fiddlesticks! Wine and tobacco rob us of our personality. After a cigar or a vodka, you're not Peter Nikoaylevitch, you're Peter Nikolayevitch plus somebody else; your ego splits up, and you begin to see yourself as a third person.

SORIN. Fine *(laughs)* for you to argue! You've lived your life, but what about me? I've served the Department of Justice twenty-eight years, but I've never lived, never seen anything, and all the rest of it, so naturally I want to have my life. You've had your fill and that's why you turn to philosophy. I want to live, and that's why I turn to sherry after dinner and smoking cigars, and so on. And that's that.

DORN. One must look seriously at life, but to go in for cures at sixty and regret the pleasures you missed in your youth, is, if you'll forgive me, frivolous.

MASHA. *(Gets up)* It must be time for lunch. *(Walking slow and hobbling)* My foot's gone to sleep. *(Exits.)*

DORN. She'll down a couple of glasses before lunch.

SORIN. The poor thing gets no happiness of her own.

DORN. Fiddlesticks, your Excellency.

SORIN. You argue like a man who's had his fill.

ARCADINA. Oh, what can be duller than this darling country dullness is! Hot, quiet, nobody ever does anything, everybody philosophises. It's good to be here with you, my friends, delightful listening to you, but—sitting in my hotel room, all by myself, studying my part—how much better!

NINA. *(Ecstatically)* Good! I understand you.

SORIN. Of course, in town's better. You sit in your study, the footman lets nobody in without announcing them, there's the telephone—on the street cabs and so on—

DORN. *(Singing sotto voce)* Tell her, my flowers—

(Enter SHAMREYEFF, behind him PAULINE.)

SHAMREYEFF. Here they are. Good morning! *(Kisses*

MADAME ARCADINA's *hand, then* NINA's) Very glad to see you looking so well. *(To* MADAME ARCADINA*)* My wife tells me you are thinking of driving into town with her today. Is that so?

ARCADINA. Yes, we are thinking of it.

SHAMREYEFF. Hm! That's magnificent, but what will you travel on, my most esteemed lady? Today around here we are hauling rye, all the hands are busy. And what horses would you take, may I ask?

ARCADINA. What horses? How should I know—what horses!

SORIN. There are carriage horses here!

SHAMREYEFF. *(Flaring up)* Carriage horses? But where do I get the harness? Where do I get the harness? It's amazing. It's incomprehensible! Most esteemed lady! Excuse me, I am on my knees before your talent, I'd gladly give ten years of my life for you, but I cannot let you have the horses!

ARCADINA. But what if I have to go? It's a fine business!

SHAMREYEFF. Most esteemed lady! You don't know what a farm means.

ARCADINA. *(Flaring up)* The same old story! In that case I'll start for Moscow today. Order me horses from the village, or I'll walk to the station.

SHAMREYEFF. *(Flaring up)* In that case I resign my position! Find yourself another steward! *(Exits.)*

ARCADINA. Every summer it's like this, every summer here they insult me! I'll never put my foot here again! *(Goes out in the direction of the bath-house.)*

(Presently she is seen going into the house. TRIGORIN *follows, with fishing rods and a pail.)*

SORIN. *(Flaring up)* This is insolent! The devil knows what it is! I'm sick of it, and so on. Bring all the horses here this very minute!

NINA. *(To* PAULINE*)* To refuse Irina Nikolayevna, the famous actress! Any little wish of hers, the least

whim, is worth more than all your farm. It's simply unbelievable!

PAULINE. *(In despair)* What can I do? Put yourself
in my shoes, what can I do?

SORIN. *(To* NINA*)* Let's go find my sister. We'll all
beg her not to leave us. Isn't that so? *(Looking in the
direction* SHAMREYEFF *went)* You insufferable man!
Tyrant!

NINA. *(Prevents his getting up)* Sit still, sit still. We'll
wheel you. *(She and* MEDVEDENKO *push the wheel chair)*
Oh, how awful it is!

SORIN. Yes, yes, it's awful. But he won't leave, I'll
speak to him right off.

(They go out. DORN *and* PAULINE *remain.)*

DORN. People are certainly tiresome. Really the thing
to do, of course, is throw that husband of yours out by
the neck; but it will all end by this old woman, Peter
Nicolayevitch, and his sister begging him to pardon them.
See if they don't.

PAULINE. He has put the carriage horses in the fields,
too. And these misunderstandings happen every day. If
you only knew how it all upsets me. It's making me ill;
you see how I'm trembling. I can't bear his coarseness.
(Entreating) Eugene my darling, light of my eyes—take
me with you. Our time is passing, we're not young any
longer; if—if only we could—for the rest of our lives
at least—stop hiding, stop pretending.

(A pause.)

DORN. I am fifty-five, it's too late to change now.

PAULINE. I know, you refuse me because there are
other women close to you. It's impossible for you to
take them all with you. I understand. I apologize! Forgive me, you are tired of me.

*(*NINA *appears before the house picking a bunch of
flowers.)*

DORN. No, not all that.

PAULINE. I am miserable with jealousy. Of course you are a doctor. You can't escape women. I understand.

DORN. *(To NINA, as she joins them)* What's happening?

NINA. Irina Nikolayevna is crying and Peter Nikolayevitch having his asthma.

DORN. *(Rising)* I must go and give them both some valerian drops.

NINA. *(Giving him the flowers)* Won't you?

DORN. *Merci bien. (Goes toward the house.)*

PAULINE. What pretty flowers! *(Nearing the house, in a low voice)* Give me those flowers! Give me those flowers!

(He hands her the flowers, she tears them to pieces and flings them away. They go into the house.)

NINA. *(Alone)* How strange it is seeing a famous actress cry, and about such a little nothing! And isn't it strange that a famous author should sit all day long fishing? The darling of the public, his name in the papers every day, his photograph for sale in shop windows, his book translated into foreign languages, and he's delighted because he's caught two chub. I imagined famous people were proud and distant, and that they despised the crowd, and used their fame and the glamor of their names to revenge themselves on the world for putting birth and money first. But here I see them crying or fishing, playing cards, laughing or losing their tempers, like everybody else.

(TREPLEFF enters, without a hat, carrying a gun and a dead sea gull.)

TREPLEFF. Are you here alone?

NINA. Alone. *(TREPLEFF lays the sea gull at her feet.)* What does that mean?

TREPLEFF. I was low enough today to kill this sea gull. I lay it at your feet.

NINA. What's the matter with you? *(Picks up sea gull and looks at it.)*

TREPLEFF. *(Pause)* It's the way I'll soon end my own life.

NINA. I don't recognize you.

TREPLEFF. Yes, ever since I stopped recognizing you. You've changed toward me. Your eyes are cold. You hate to have me near you.

NINA. You are so irritable lately, and you talk—it's as if you were talking in symbols. And this sea gull, I suppose that's a symbol, too. Forgive me, but I don't understand it. *(Lays the sea gull on the seat)* I'm too simple to understand you.

TREPLEFF. This began that evening when my play failed so stupidly. Women will never forgive failure. I've burnt it all, every scrap of it. If you only knew what I'm going through! Your growing cold to me is terrible, unbelievable; it's as if I had suddenly waked and found this lake dried up and sunk in the ground. You say you are too simple to understand me. Oh, what is there to understand? My play didn't catch your fancy, you despise my kind of imagination, you already consider me commonplace, insignificant, like so many others. *(Stamping his foot)* How well I understand it all, how I understand it. It's like a spike in my brain, may it be damned along with my pride, which is sucking my blood, sucking it like a snake. *(He sees TRIGORIN, who enters reading a book)* Here comes the real genius, he walks like Hamlet, and with a book too. *(Mimicking)* "Words, words, words." This sun has hardly reached you, and you are already smiling, your glance is melting in his rays. I won't stand in your way. *(He goes out.)*

TRIGORIN. *(Making notes in a book)* Takes snuff and drinks vodka, always wears black. The schoolmaster in love with her.

NINA. Good morning, Boris Alexeyevitch!

TRIGORIN. Good morning. It seems that things have

taken a turn we hadn't expected, so we are leaving today. You and I aren't likely to meet again. I'm sorry. I don't often meet young women, young and charming. I've forgotten how one feels at eighteen or nineteen, I can't picture it very clearly, and so the girls I draw in my stories and novels are mostly wrong. I'd like to be in your shoes for just one hour, to see things through your eyes, and find out just what sort of a little person you are.

NINA. And how I'd like to be in your shoes!

TRIGORIN. Why?

NINA. To know how it feels being a famous genius. What's it like being famous? How does it make you feel?

TRIGORIN. How? Nohow, I should think. I'd never thought about it. *(Reflecting)* One of two things: either you exaggerate my fame, or else my fame hasn't made me feel it.

NINA. But if you read about yourself in the papers?

TRIGORIN. When they praise me I'm pleased; when they abuse me, I feel whipped for a day or so.

NINA. It's a marvelous world! If you only knew how I envy you! Look how different different people's lots are! Some have all they can do to drag through their dull, obscure lives; they are all just alike, all miserable; others—well, you for instance—have a bright, interesting life that means something. You are happy.

TRIGORIN. I? *(Shrugging his shoulders)* H'm—I hear you speak of fame and happiness, of a bright, interesting life, but for me that's all words, pretty words that—if you'll forgive my saying so—mean about the same to me as candied fruits, which I never eat. You are very young and very kind.

NINA. Your life is beautiful.

TRIGORIN. I don't see anything so very beautiful about it. *(Looks at his watch)* I must get to my writing. Excuse me, I'm busy— *(Laughs)* You've stepped on my pet corn, as they say, and here I am, beginning to get excited and a little cross. At any rate let's talk. Let's talk about my beautiful, bright life. Well, where shall we begin? *(After reflecting a moment)* You know, sometimes violent obsessions take hold of a man, some fixed idea pursues him, the moon for example, day and night he thinks of nothing but the moon. Well, I have just such a moon. Day and night one thought obsesses me: I must be writing, I must be writing, I must be— I've scarcely finished one novel when somehow I'm driven on to write another, then a third, and after the third a fourth. I write incessantly, and always at a breakneck speed, and that's the only way I can write. What's beautiful and bright about that, I ask you? Oh, what a wild life! Why now even, I'm here talking to you, I'm excited, but every minute I remember that the story I haven't finished is there waiting for me. I see that cloud up there, it's shaped like a grand piano—instantly a mental note—I must remember to put that in my story —a cloud sailing by—grand piano. A whiff of heliotrope. Quickly I make note of it: cloying smell, widow's color —put that in next time I describe a summer evening. Every sentence, every word I say and you say, I lie in wait for it, snap it up for my literary storeroom—it might come in handy— As soon as I put my work down, I race off to the theatre or go fishing, hoping to find a rest, but not at all—a new idea for a story comes rolling around in my head like a cannon ball, and I'm back at my desk, and writing and writing and writing. And it's always like that, everlastingly. I have no rest from myself, and I feel that I am consuming my own life, that for the honey I'm giving to someone in the void, I rob my best flowers of their pollen, I tear up those flowers and trample on their roots. Do I seem mad? Do my friends seem to talk with me as they would to a sane man? "What are you writing at now? What shall we have next?" Over and over it's like that, till I think all this attention and praise is said only out of kindness to a sick man—deceive him, soothe him, and then any minute come stealing up behind and pack him off to the madhouse. And in those years, my young best years, when I was beginning, why then writing made my life a torment. A minor writer, especially when he's not successful, feels clumsy, he's all thumbs, the world has no need for him; his nerves are about to go; he can't resist hanging around people in the arts, where nobody knows him, or take any notice of him, and he's afraid to look them straight in the eyes, like a man with a passion for gambling who hasn't any money to play with. I'd never seen my readers but for some reason or other I pictured them as hating me and mistrusting me, I had a deathly fear of the public, and when my first play was produced it seemed to me all the dark eyes in the audience were looking at it with hostility and all the light eyes with frigid indifference. Oh how awful that was! What torment it was!

NINA. But surely the inspiration you feel and the creation itself of something must give you a moment of high, sweet happiness, don't they?

TRIGORIN. Yes. When I'm writing I enjoy it and I enjoy reading my proofs, but the minute it comes out I detest it; I see it's not what I meant it to be; I was wrong to write it at all, and I'm vexed and sick at heart about it. *(Laughs)* Then the public reads it. "Yes, charming, clever—Charming but nothing like Tolstoy: A very fine thing, but Turgenev's 'Fathers and Sons' is finer." To my dying day that's what it will be, clever and charming, charming and clever—nothing more. And when I'm dead they'll be saying at my grave, "Here lies Trigorin, a delightful writer but not so good as Turgenev."

NINA. Excuse me, but I refuse to understand you. You are simply spoiled by success.

TRIGORIN. What success? I have never pleased myself. I don't like myself as a writer. The worst of it is that I am in a sort of daze and often don't understand what I write—I love this water here, the trees, the sky, I feel nature, it stirs in me a passion, an irresistible desire to write. But I am not only a landscape painter, I am a citizen too, I love my country, the people, I feel that if I am a writer I ought to speak also of the people, of their sufferings, of their future, speak of science, of the rights of man, and so forth, and I speak of everything, I hurry up, on all sides they are after me, are annoyed at me, I dash from side to side like a fox the hounds are baiting, I see life and science getting always farther and farther ahead as I fall always more and more behind, like a peasant, missing his train, and the upshot is I feel that I can write only landscape, and in all the rest I am false and false to the marrow of my bones.

NINA. You work too hard, and have no time and no wish to feel your own importance. You may be dissatisfied with yourself, of course, but other people think you are great and excellent. If I were such a writer as you are I'd give my whole life to the people, but I should feel that the only happiness for them would be in rising to me; and they should draw my chariot.

TRIGORIN. Well, in a chariot—Agamemnon am I, or what?

(They BOTH *smile.)*

NINA. For the happiness of being an author or an actress I would bear any poverty, disillusionment, I'd have people hate me. I'd live in a garret and eat black bread, I'd endure my own dissatisfaction with myself and all my faults, but in return I should ask for fame —real resounding fame. *(Covers her face with her hands)* My head's swimming— Ouf!

ARCADINA. *(From within the house)* Boris Alexeye-vitch!

TRIGORIN. She's calling me. I dare say, to come and pack. But I don't feel like going away. *(He glances at the lake)* Look, how beautiful it is! Marvelous!

NINA. Do you see over there that house and garden?

TRIGORIN. Yes.

NINA. It used to belong to my dear mother. I was born there. I've spent all my life by this lake and I know every little island on it.

TRIGORIN. It's all very charming. *(Seeing the sea gull)* What is that?

NINA. A sea gull. Constantine shot it.

TRIGORIN. It's a lovely bird. Really, I don't want to leave here. Do try and persuade Irina Nikolayevna to stay. *(Makes a note in his book.)*

NINA. What is it you're writing?

TRIGORIN. Only a note. An idea struck me. *(Putting the notebook away)* An idea for a short story: a young girl, one like you, has lived all her life beside a lake; she loves the lake like a sea gull and is happy and free like a sea gull. But by chance a man comes, sees her, and out of nothing better to do, destroys her, like this sea gull here.

(A pause. MADAME ARCADINA appears at the window.)

ARCADINA. Boris Alexeyevitch, where are you?

TRIGORIN. Right away! *(Goes toward the house, looking back at NINA. MADAME ARCADINA remains at the window.)* What is it?

ARCADINA. We're staying.

(TRIGORIN enters the house.)

NINA. *(Coming forward, standing lost in thought)* It's a dream!

CURTAIN

ACT THREE

The dining-room in SORIN'S *house. On the Right and
Left are doors. A sideboard. A medicine cupboard.
In the middle of the room a table. A small trunk and
hat-boxes, signs of preparations for leaving.*

TRIGORIN *is at lunch,* MASHA *standing by the
table.*

MASHA. I tell you this because you're a writer. You
might use it. I tell you the truth: if he had died when he
shot himself I wouldn't live another minute. Just the
same I'm getting braver; I've just made up my mind to
tear this love out of my heart by the roots.

TRIGORIN. How will you do it?

MASHA. I'm going to get married. To Medvedenko.

TRIGORIN. Is that the schoolmaster?

MASHA. Yes.

TRIGORIN. I don't see why you must do that.

MASHA. Loving without hope, waiting the whole year
long for something—but when I'm married I won't have
any time for love, there'll be plenty of new things I'll
have to do to make me forget the past. Anyhow it will
be a change, you know. Shall we have another?

TRIGORIN. Haven't you had about enough?

MASHA. Ah! *(Pours two glasses)* Here! Don't look
at me like that! Women drink oftener than you imagine.
Not so many of them drink openly like me. Most of
them hide it. Yes. And it's always vodka or cognac.
(Clinks glasses) Your health. You're a decent sort, I'm
sorry to be parting from you.

(They drink.)

33

TRIGORIN. I don't want to leave here myself.

MASHA. You should beg her to stay.

TRIGORIN. She'd never do that now. Her son is be-having himself very tactlessly. First he tries shooting himself and now, they say, he's going to challenge me to a duel. But what for? He sulks, he snorts, he preaches new art forms—but there's room for all, the new and the old—why elbow?

MASHA. Well, and there's jealousy. However, that's not my business.

(Pause. YAKOV crosses Right to Left with a piece of luggage. NINA enters, stops near window.)

MASHA. That schoolmaster of mine is none too clever, but he's a good man and he's poor, and he loves me dearly. I'm sorry for him and I'm sorry for his old mother. Well, let me wish you every happiness. Think kindly of me. *(Warmly shakes his hand)* Let me thank you for your friendly interest. Send me your books, be sure to write in them. Only don't put "esteemed lady," but simply this: "To Marya, who not remembering her origin, does not know why she is living in this world." Goodbye. *(Goes out.)*

NINA. *(Holding out her hand closed to* TRIGORIN) Even or odd?

TRIGORIN. Even.

NINA. *(Sighing)* No. I had only one pea in my hand. I was trying my fortune: To be an actress or not. I wish somebody would advise me.

TRIGORIN. There's no advice in this sort of thing.

(A pause.)

NINA. We are going to part—I may never see you again. Won't you take this little medal to remember me? I've had it engraved with your initials and on the other side the title of your book: *Days and Nights.*

TRIGORIN. What a graceful thing to do! *(Kisses the medal)* It's a charming present.

NINA. Sometimes think of me.

TRIGORIN. I'll think of you. I'll think of you as I saw you that sunny day—do you remember—a week ago when you had on your white dress—we were talking—a white sea gull was lying on the bench beside us.

NINA. *(Pensive)* Yes, the sea gull. *(A pause)* Some one's coming—let me see you two minutes before you go, won't you? *(Goes out on the Left as* MADAME ARCADINA *and* SORIN, *in full dress, with a decoration, enter, then* YAKOV, *busy with the packing.)*

ARCADINA. Stay at home, old man. How could you be running about with your rheumatism? *(To* TRIGORIN) Who was it just went out? Nina?

TRIGORIN. Yes.

ARCADINA. *Pardon!* We intruded. *(Sits down)* I believe everything's packed. I'm exhausted.

TRIGORIN. *Days and Nights,* page 121, lines eleven and twelve.

YAKOV. *(Clearing the table)* Shall I pack your fishing rods as well?

TRIGORIN. Yes, I'll want them again. But the books you can give away.

YAKOV. Yes, sir.

TRIGORIN. *(To himself)* Page 121, lines eleven and twelve. What's in those lines? *(To* ARCADINA) Have you my works here in the house?

ARCADINA. Yes, in my brother's study, the corner bookcase.

TRIGORIN. Page 121. *(Exits.)*

ARCADINA. Really, Petrusha, you'd better stay at home.

SORIN. You're going away. It's dreary for me here at home without you.

ARCADINA. But what's there in town?

SORIN. Nothing in particular, but all the same. *(Laughs)* There's the laying of the foundation stone for the town hall, and all that sort of thing. A man longs if

only for an hour or so to get out of this gudgeon existence, and it's much too long I've been lying around like
an old cigarette holder. I've ordered the horses around
at one o'clock, we'll set off at the same time.

ARCADINA. *(After a pause)* Oh, stay here, don't be
lonesome, don't take cold. Look after my son. Take care
of him. Advise him. *(A pause)* Here I am leaving and
so shall never know why Constantine tried to kill himself. I have a notion the main reason was jealousy, and
the sooner I take Trigorin away from here the better.

SORIN. How should I explain it to you? There were
other reasons beside jealousy. Here we have a man who
is young, intelligent, living in the country in solitude,
without money, without position, without a future. He
has nothing to do. He is ashamed and afraid of his idle-
ness. I love him very much and he's attached to me, but
he feels just the same that he's superfluous in this house,
and a sort of dependent here, a poor relation. That's
something we can understand, it's pride of course.

ARCADINA. I'm worried about him. *(Reflecting)* He
might go into the service, perhaps.

SORIN. *(Whistling, then hesitatingly)* It seems to me
the best thing you could do would be to let him have a
little money. In the first place he ought to be able to
dress himself like other people, and so on. Look how
he's worn that same old jacket these past three years; he
runs around without an overcoat. *(Laughs)* Yes, and it
wouldn't harm him to have a little fun—he might go
abroad, perhaps—it wouldn't cost much.

ARCADINA. Perhaps I could manage a suit, but as for
going abroad—no. Just at this moment I can't even manage the suit. *(Firmly)* I haven't any money! (SORIN
laughs.) I haven't. No.

SORIN. *(Whistling)* Very well. Forgive me, my dear,
don't be angry. You're a generous, noble woman.

ARCADINA. *(Weeping)* I haven't any money.

SORIN. Of course if I had any money, I'd give him
some myself, but I haven't anything, not a kopek.

(Laughs) My manager takes all my pension and spends it on agriculture, cattle-raising, bee-keeping, and my money goes for nothing. The bees die, the cows die, horses they never let me have.

ARCADINA. Yes, I have some money, but I'm an actress, my costumes alone are enough to ruin me.

SORIN. You are very good, my dear. I respect you. Yes— But there again something's coming over me— *(Staggers)* My head's swimming. *(Leans on table)* I feel faint, and so on.

ARCADINA. *(Alarmed)* Petrusha! *(Trying to support him)* Petrusha, my darling! *(Calls)* Help me! Help!

(Enter TREPLEFF, *his head bandaged, and* MEDVEDENKO.)

ARCADINA. He feels faint.

SORIN. It's nothing, it's nothing— *(Smiles and drinks water)* It's gone already—and so on.

TREPLEFF. *(To his mother)* Don't be alarmed, Mother, it's not serious. It often happens now to my uncle. Uncle, you must lie down a little.

SORIN. A little, yes. All the same I'm going to town— I'm lying down a little and I'm going to town—that's clear. *(He goes, leaning on his stick.)*

MEDVEDENKO. *(Gives him his arm)* There's a riddle: in the morning it's on four legs, at noon on two, in the evening on three.

SORIN. *(Laughs)* That's it. And on the back at night. Thank you, I can manage alone.

MEDVEDENKO. My, what ceremony! *(He and* SORIN *go out.)*

ARCADINA. How he frightened me!

TREPLEFF. It's not good for him to live in the country. He's low in his mind. Now, Mother, if you'd only have a burst of sudden generosity and lend him a thousand or fifteen hundred, he could spend a whole year in town.

ARCADINA. I haven't any money. I'm an actress, not a banker.

(A pause.)

TREPLEFF. Mother, change my bandage. You do it so well.

ARCADINA. *(Takes bottle of iodoform and a box of bandages from cupboard)* And the doctor's late.

TREPLEFF. He promised to be here at ten, but it's already noon.

ARCADINA. Sit down. *(Takes off bandage)* You look as if you were in a turban. Some man who came by the kitchen yesterday asked what nationality you were. But it's almost entirely healed. What's left is nothing. *(Kisses him on the head)* While I'm away, you won't do any more click-click?

TREPLEFF. No, Mother. That was a moment when I was out of my head with despair, and couldn't control myself. It won't happen again. *(Kisses her fingers)* You have clever fingers. I remember long, long ago when you were still playing at the Imperial Theatre—there was a fight one day in our court, and a washerwoman who was one of the tenants got beaten almost to death. Do you remember? She was picked up unconscious—you nursed her, took medicines to her, bathed her children in the washtub. Don't you remember?

ARCADINA. No. *(Puts on fresh bandage.)*

TREPLEFF. Two ballet dancers were living then in the same house we did, they used to come and drink coffee with you.

ARCADINA. That I remember.

TREPLEFF. They were very pious. *(A pause.)* Lately, these last days, I have loved you as tenderly and fully as when I was a child. Except for you, there's nobody left me now. Only why, why do you subject yourself to the influence of that man?

ARCADINA. You don't understand him, Constantine. He's a very noble character.

TREPLEFF. Nevertheless, when he was told I was going to challenge him to a duel, nobility didn't keep him from playing the coward. He's leaving. Ignominious retreat!

ARCADINA. Such tosh! I myself beg him to leave here.

TREPLEFF. Noble character! Here we both are nearly quarreling over him, and right now very likely he's in the drawing-room or in the garden laughing at us—developing Nina, trying once and for all to convince her he's a genius.

ARCADINA. For you it's a pleasure—saying disagreeable things to me. I respect that man and must ask you not to speak ill of him in my presence.

TREPLEFF. And I don't respect him. You want me too to think he's a genius, but, forgive me, I can't tell lies—his creations make me sick.

ARCADINA. That's envy. People who are not talented but pretend to be have nothing better to do than to disparage real talents. It must be a fine consolation!

TREPLEFF. *(Sarcastically)* Real talents! *(Angrily)* I'm more talented than both of you put together, if it comes to that! *(Tears off the bandage)* You two, with your stale routine, have grabbed first place in art and think that only what you do is real or legitimate; the rest you'd like to stifle and keep down. I don't believe in you two. I don't believe in you or in him.

ARCADINA. Decadent!

TREPLEFF. Go back to your darling theatre and act there in trashy, stupid plays!

ARCADINA. Never did I act in such plays. Leave me alone! You are not fit to write even wretched vaudeville. Kiev burgher! Sponge!

TREPLEFF. Miser!

ARCADINA. Beggar! *(He sits down, cries softly.)* Nonentity! *(Walks up and down)* Don't cry! You mustn't cry! *(Weeps. Kisses him on his forehead, his cheeks, his head)* My dear child, forgive me! Forgive me, your wicked mother! Forgive miserable me!

TREPLEFF. *(Embracing her)* If you only knew! I've lost everything. She doesn't love me, now I can't write. All my hopes are gone.

ARCADINA. Don't despair. It will all pass. He's leaving right away. She'll love you again. *(Dries his tears)* That's enough. We've made it up now.

TREPLEFF. *(Kissing her hands)* Yes, Mother.

ARCADINA. *(Tenderly)* Make it up with him, too. You don't want a duel. You don't, do you?

TREPLEFF. Very well, only, Mother, don't let me see him. It's painful to me. It's beyond me. (TRIGORIN *comes in.)* There he is. I'm going. *(Quickly puts dressings away in cupboard)* The doctor will do my bandage later.

TRIGORIN. *(Looking through a book)* Page 121—lines eleven and twelve. Here it is. *(Reads)* "If you ever, ever need my life, come and take it."

(TREPLEFF *picks up the bandage from the floor and goes out.)*

ARCADINA. *(Looking at her watch)* The horses will be here soon.

TRIGORIN. *(To himself)* If you ever, ever need my life, come and take it.

ARCADINA. I hope you are all packed.

TRIGORIN. *(Impatiently)* Yes, yes— *(In deep thought)* Why is it I thought I felt sadness in that call from a pure soul, and my heart aches so with pity? If you ever, ever need my life, come and take it. *(To* MADAME ARCADINA) Let's stay just one more day. *(She shakes her head.)*

TRIGORIN. Let's stay!

ARCADINA. Darling, I know what keeps you here. But have some self control. You're a little drunk, be sober.

TRIGORIN. You be sober, too, be understanding, reasonable, I beg you; look at all this like a true friend— *(Presses her hand)* You are capable of sacrificing. Be my friend, let me be free.

ARCADINA. *(Excited)* Are you so infatuated?

TRIGORIN. I am drawn to her! Perhaps this is just what I need.

ARCADINA. The love of some provincial girl? Oh, how little you know yourself!

TRIGORIN. Sometimes people talk but are asleep. That's how it is now—I'm talking to you but in my dream see her. I'm possessed by sweet, marvelous dreams. Let me go—

ARCADINA. *(Trembling)* No, no, I'm an ordinary woman like any other woman, you shouldn't talk to me like this. Don't torture me, Boris. It frightens me.

TRIGORIN. If you wanted to, you could be far from ordinary. There is a kind of love that's young, and beautiful, and is all poetry, and carries us away into a world of dreams; on earth it alone can ever give us happiness. Such a love I still have never known. In my youth there wasn't time, I was always around some editor's office, fighting off starvation. Now it's here, that love, it's come, it beckons me. What sense, then, is there in running away from it?

ARCADINA. *(Angry)* You've gone mad.

TRIGORIN. Well, let me!

ARCADINA. You've all conspired today just to torment me. *(Weeps.)*

TRIGORIN. *(Clutching at his breast)* She doesn't understand. She doesn't want to understand.

ARCADINA. Am I so old or ugly that you don't mind talking to me about other women? *(Embracing and kissing him)* Oh, you madman! My beautiful, my marvel— you are the last chapter of my life. *(Falls on knees)* My joy, my pride, my blessedness! *(Embracing his knees)* If you forsake me for one hour even, I'll never survive it, I'll go out of my mind, my wonderful, magnificent one, my master.

TRIGORIN. Somebody might come in. *(Helps her to rise.)*

ARCADINA. Let them, I am not ashamed of my love for you. *(Kisses his hands)* My treasure! You reckless boy, you want to be mad, but I won't have it, I won't let you. *(Laughs)* You are mine—you are mine. This brow is mine, and the eyes mine, and this beautiful silky hair, too, is mine. You are all mine. You are so talented, so intelligent, the best of all modern writers; you are the one and only hope of Russia—you have such sincerity, simplicity, healthy humor. In one stroke you go to the very heart of a character or a scene; your people are like life itself. Oh, it's impossible to read you without rapture! Do you think this is only incense? I'm flattering you? Come, look me in the eyes— Do I look like a liar? There you see, only I can appreciate you; only I tell you the truth, my lovely darling.—You are coming? Yes? You won't leave me?

TRIGORIN. I have no will of my own—I've never had a will of my own. Flabby, weak, always submitting! Is it possible that might please women? Take me, carry me away, only never let me be one step away from you.

ARCADINA. *(To herself)* Now he's mine. *(Casually, as if nothing had happened)* However, if you like you may stay. I'll go by myself, and you come later, in a week. After all, where would you hurry to?

TRIGORIN. No, let's go together.

ARCADINA. As you like. Together, together then. *(A pause.* TRIGORIN *writes in notebook.)* What are you writing?

TRIGORIN. This morning I heard a happy expression: "Virgin forest." It might be useful in a story. *(Yawns)* So, we're off. Once more the cars, stations, station buffets, stews and conversations!

(SHAMREYEFF *enters.)*

SHAMREYEFF. I have the honor with deep regret to announce that the horses are ready. It's time, most esteemed lady, to be off to the station; the train arrives at five minutes after two. So will you do me the favor, Irina Nikolayevna, not to forget to inquire about this: Where's the actor Suzdaltsev now? Is he alive? Is he well? We used to drink together once upon a time. In "The Stolen Mail" he was inimitable. In the same company with him at Elisavetgrad, I remember, was the tragedian Izmailov, also a remarkable personality. Don't hurry, most esteemed lady, there are five minutes still. Once in some melodrama they were playing conspirators, and when they were suddenly discovered, he had to say "we are caught in a trap," but Izmailov said, "We are traught in a clap." *(Laughs)* Clap!

(YAKOV *is busy with luggage.* MAID *brings* ARCADINA'S *hat, coat, parasol, gloves.* ALL *help her put them on. The* COOK *peers through door on Left, as if hesitating, then he comes in. Enter* PAULINE, SORIN *and* MEDVEDENKO.)

PAULINE. *(With basket)* Here are some plums for the journey. They are sweet ones. In case you'd like some little thing.

ARCADINA. You are very kind, Pauline Andreyevna.

PAULINE. Goodbye, my dear: If anything has been not quite so, forgive it. *(Cries.)*

ARCADINA. *(Embracing her)* Everything has been charming, everything's been charming. Only you mustn't cry.

PAULINE. Time goes so.

ARCADINA. There's nothing we can do about that.

SORIN. *(In a great coat with a cape, his hat on and his stick in his hand, crossing the stage)* Sister, you'd better start if you don't want to be late. I'll go get in the carriage. *(Exits.)*

MEDVEDENKO. And I'll walk to the station—to see you off. I'll step lively.

ARCADINA. Goodbye, my friends. If we are alive and well next summer we'll meet again. *(The* MAID, COOK *and* YAKOV *kiss her hand.)* Don't forget me. *(Gives* COOK *a rouble)* Here's a rouble for the three of you.

COOK. We humbly thank you, Madam. Pleasant journey to you. Many thanks to you.

YAKOV. God bless you!

SHAMREYEFF. Make us happy with a letter. Goodbye, Boris Alexeyevitch.

ARCADINA. Where's Constantine? Tell him I'm off now. I must say goodbye to him. Well, remember me kindly. *(To* YAKOV) I gave the cook a rouble. It's for the three of you.

*(*ALL *go out. The stage is empty. Off-stage are heard the usual sounds when people are going away. The* MAID *comes back for the basket of plums from the table and goes out again.)*

TRIGORIN. *(Returning)* I forgot my stick. It's out there on the terrace, I think. *(As he starts to go out by the door on the Left, he meets* NINA *coming in)* Is it you? We are just going—

NINA. I felt we should meet again. *(Excited)* Boris Alexeyevitch, I've come to a decision, the die is cast. I am going on the stage. Tomorrow I shall not be here. I am leaving my father, deserting everything, beginning a new life. I'm off like you—for Moscow—we shall meet there.

TRIGORIN. *(Glancing around him)* Stay at Hotel Slavyansky Bazaar. Let me know at once. Molchanovka, Groholsky House. I must hurry.

(A pause.)

NINA. One minute yet.

TRIGORIN. *(In a low voice)* You are so beautiful— Oh, how happy to think we'll be meeting soon. *(She puts her head on his breast)* I shall see those lovely eyes again, that ineffably beautiful, tender smile—those gentle features, their pure, angelic expression—my darling—

(A long kiss.)

CURTAIN

(Two years pass between the Third and Fourth Acts.)

ACT FOUR

One of the drawing-rooms in SORIN'S *house, turned by*
CONSTANTINE TREPLEFF *into a study. On the Right
and Left, doors leading into other parts of the
house. Facing us, glass doors on to the terrace.
Beside the usual furniture of a drawing-room, there
is a writing-table in the corner to the Right; near
the door on the Left, a sofa, a book-case full of
books, and books in the windows and on the chairs.*

*Evening. A single lamp with a shade is lighted. Semi-
darkness. The sound from outside of trees rustling
and the wind howling in the chimney. The night
watchman is knocking.* MEDVEDENKO *and* MASHA
come in.

MASHA. Constantine Gavrilovitch! Constantine Gavrilovitch! *(Looking around)* Nobody here. Every other
minute all day long the old man keeps asking where's
Kostya, where's Kostya? He can't live without him.

MEDVEDENKO. He's afraid to be alone. *(Listening)*
What terrible weather! It's two days now.

MASHA. *(Turning up the lamp)* Out on the lake there
are waves. Tremendous.

MEDVEDENKO. The garden's black. We ought to have
told them to pull down that stage. It stands all bare and
hideous, like a skeleton, and the curtain flaps in the wind.
When I passed there last night it seemed to me that in
the wind I heard some one crying.

MASHA. Well, here— *(Pause.)*

MEDVEDENKO. Masha, let's go home.

MASHA. *(Shakes her head)* I'm going to stay here
tonight.

45

MEDVEDENKO. *(Imploring)* Masha, let's go. Our baby must be hungry.

MASHA. Nonsense. Matriona will feed it.

(A pause.)

MEDVEDENKO. It's hard on him. He's been three nights now without his mother.

MASHA. You're getting just too tiresome. In the old days you'd at least philosophize a little, but now it's all baby, home, baby, home—and that's all I can get out of you.

MEDVEDENKO. Let's go, Masha.

MASHA. Go yourself.

MEDVEDENKO. Your father won't let me have a horse.

MASHA. He will if you just ask him.

MEDVEDENKO. Very well, I'll try. Then you'll come tomorrow.

MASHA. *(Taking snuff)* Well, tomorrow. Stop bothering me.

(Enter TREPLEFF *and* PAULINE; TREPLEFF *carries pillows and a blanket,* PAULINE *sheets and pillow cases. They lay them on the sofa, then* TREPLEFF *goes and sits down at his desk.)*

MASHA. Why's that, Mama?

PAULINE. Peter Nikolayevitch asked to sleep in Kostya's room.

MASHA. Let me— *(She makes the bed.)*

PAULINE. *(Sighing)* Old people, what children— *(Goes to the desk. Leaning on her elbows she gazes at the manuscript. A pause.)*

MEDVEDENKO. So I'm going. Goodbye, Masha. *(Kisses her hand)* Goodbye, Mother. *(Tries to kiss her hand.)*

PAULINE. *(With annoyance)* Well, go if you're going.

MEDVEDENKO. Goodbye, Constantine Gavrilovitch.

(TREPLEFF *without speaking gives him his hand.*
MEDVEDENKO *goes out.*)

PAULINE. *(Gazing at the manuscript)* Nobody ever
thought or dreamed that some day, Kostya, you'd turn
out to be a real author. But now, thank God, the mag-
azines send you money for your stories. *(Passing her
hand over his hair)* And you've grown handsome—dear,
good Kostya, be kind to my little Masha.

MASHA. *(Making the bed)* Let him alone, Mama.

PAULINE. She's a sweet little thing. *(A pause)* A
woman, Kostya, doesn't ask much—only kind looks. As
I well know.

(TREPLEFF *rises from the desk and without speaking
goes out.*)

MASHA. You shouldn't have bothered him.

PAULINE. I feel sorry for you, Masha.

MASHA. Why should you?

PAULINE. My heart aches and aches for you. I see it
all, I understand everything.

MASHA. It's all foolishness! Hopeless love—that's
only in novels. No matter. Only you mustn't let yourself
go, and be always waiting for something, waiting for
fine weather by the sea. If love stirs in your heart, stamp
it out. Now they've promised to transfer my husband to
another district. As soon as we get there—I'll forget it
all—I'll tear it out of my heart by the roots.

(Two rooms off is heard a melancholy waltz.)

PAULINE. Kostya is playing. That means he's feeling
sad.

MASHA. *(Waltzes silently a few turns)* The great
thing, Mama, is to be where I don't see him. If only my
Semyon could get his transfer, I promise you I'd forget
in a month. It's all nonsense.

(Door on Left opens. DORN *and* MEDVEDENKO *come in,
wheeling* SORIN *in his chair.)*

MEDVEDENKO. I have six souls at home now. And flour at seventy kopeks.

DORN. So it just goes round and round.

MEDVEDENKO. It's easy for you to smile. You've got more money than the chickens could pick up.

DORN. Money! After practicing medicine thirty years, my friend, so driven day and night that I could never call my soul my own, I managed to save up at last two thousand rubles; and I've just spent all that on a trip abroad. I've got nothing at all.

MASHA. *(To her husband)* Aren't you gone yet?

MEDVEDENKO. *(Apologizing)* How can I, when they won't let me have a horse?

MASHA. *(Under her breath angrily)* I wish I'd never lay eyes on you again.

(SORIN'S *wheel-chair remains Left Center.* PAULINE, MASHA *and* DORN *sit down beside him.* MEDVE-DENKO *stands to one side gloomily.)*

DORN. Look how many changes they have made here! The drawing-room is turned into a study.

MASHA. Constantine Gavrilovitch likes to work in here. He can go into the garden whenever he likes and think.

(A watchman's rattle sounds.)

SORIN. Where's my sister?

DORN. She went to the station to meet Trigorin. She'll be right back.

SORIN. If you thought you had to send for my sister, that shows I'm very ill. *(Reflecting)* Now that's odd, isn't it? I'm very ill, but they won't let me have any medicine around here.

DORN. And what would you like? Valerian drops? Soda? Quinine?

SORIN. So it's more philosophy, I suppose. Oh, what an affliction! *(He motions with his head toward the sofa)* Is that for me?

PAULINE. Yes, for you, Peter Nikolayevitch.

SORIN. Thank you.

DORN. *(Singing sotto voce)* The moon drifts in the sky tonight.

SORIN. Listen, I want to give Kostya a subject for a story. It should be called: "The Man Who Wanted To" —*L'homme qui a voulu*. In my youth long ago wanted to become an author—and never became one; wanted to speak eloquently—and spoke execrably *(mimicking himself)* and so on and so forth, and all the rest of it, yes and no, and in the résumé would drag on, drag on, till the sweat broke out; wanted to marry—and never married; wanted always to live in town—and now am ending up my life in the country, and so on.

DORN. Wanted to become a State Counsellor—and became one.

SORIN. *(Laughing)* For that I never longed. That came to me of itself.

DORN. Come now, to be picking faults with life at sixty-two, you must confess, that's not magnanimous.

SORIN. How bullheaded you are! Can't you take it in? I want to live.

DORN. That's frivolous, it's the law of nature that every life must come to an end.

SORIN. You argue like a man who's had his fill. You've had your fill and so you're indifferent to living, it's all one to you. But at that even you will be afraid to die.

DORN. The fear of death—a brute fear. We must overcome it. The fear of death is reasonable only in those who believe in an eternal life, and shudder to think of the sins they have committed. But you in the first place don't believe, in the second place what sins have you? For twenty-five years you served as State Counsellor—and that's all.

SORIN. *(Laughing)* Twenty-eight.

(TREPLEFF *enters and sits on the stool beside* SORIN. MASHA *never takes her eyes off his face.)*

DORN. We are keeping Constantine Gavrilovitch from his work.

TREPLEFF. No, it's nothing.

(A pause.)

MEDVEDENKO. Permit me to ask you, Doctor, what town in your travels did you most prefer?

DORN. Genoa.

TREPLEFF. Why Genoa?

DORN. Because of the marvelous street crowd. When you go out of your hotel in the evening you find the whole street surging with people. You let yourself drift among the crowd, zig-zagging back and forth, you live its life, its soul pours into you, until finally you begin to believe there might really be a world spirit after all, like that Nina Zaretchny acted in your play. By the way, where is Nina just now? Where is she and how is she?

TREPLEFF. Very well, I imagine.

DORN. I've been told she was leading rather an odd sort of life. How's that?

TREPLEFF. It's a long story, Doctor.

DORN. You can shorten it.

(A pause.)

TREPLEFF. She ran away from home and joined Trigorin. That you knew?

DORN. I know.

TREPLEFF. She had a child. The child died. Trigorin got tired of her, and went back to his old ties, as might be expected. He'd never broken these old ties anyhow, but flitted in that backboneless style of his from one to the other. As far as I could say from what I know, Nina's private life didn't quite work out.

DORN. And on the stage?

TREPLEFF. I believe even worse. She made her debut in Moscow at a summer theatre, and afterward a tour in the provinces. At that time I never let her out of my sight, and wherever she was I was. She always attempted big parts, but her acting was crude, without any taste, her gestures were clumsy. There were moments when she did some talented screaming, talented dying, but those were only moments.

DORN. It means, though, she has talent?

TREPLEFF. I could never make out. I imagine she has. I saw her, but she didn't want to see me, and her maid wouldn't let me in her rooms. I understood how she felt, and never insisted on seeing her. *(A pause.)* What more is there to tell you? Afterward, when I'd come back home here, she wrote me some letters. They were clever, tender, interesting; she didn't complain, but I could see she was profoundly unhappy; there was not a word that didn't show her exhausted nerves. And she'd taken a strange fancy. She always signed herself the sea gull. In "The Mermaid" the miller says that he's a crow; the same way in all her letters she kept repeating she was a sea gull. Now she's here.

DORN. How do you mean, here?

TREPLEFF. In town, staying at the inn. She's already been here five days, living there in rooms. Masha drove in, but she never sees anybody. Semyon Semyonovich declares that last night after dinner he saw her in the fields, a mile and a half from here.

MEDVEDENKO. Yes, I saw her. *(A pause.)* Going in the opposite direction from here, toward town. I bowed to her, asked why she had not been out to see us. She said she'd come.

TREPLEFF. Well, she won't. *(A pause.)* Her father and stepmother don't want to know her. They've set watchmen to keep her off the grounds. *(Goes toward the desk with* DORN*)* How easy it is, Doctor, to be a philosopher on paper, and how hard it is in life!

SORIN. She was a beautiful girl.

DORN. How's that?

SORIN. I say she was a beautiful girl. State Counsellor Sorin was downright in love with her himself once for a while.

DORN. You old Lovelace!

(They hear SHAMREYEFF's *laugh.)*

PAULINE. I imagine they're back from the station.
TREPLEFF. Yes, I hear Mother.

(Enter MADAME ARCADINA *and* TRIGORIN, SHAMREY-
EFF *following.)*

SHAMREYEFF. We all get old and fade with the ele-
ments, esteemed lady, but you, most honored lady, are
still young—white dress, vivacity—grace.
ARCADINA. You still want to bring me bad luck, you
tiresome creature!
TRIGORIN. *(To* SORIN) Howdy do, Peter Nikolaye-
vitch. How is it you are still indisposed? That's not so
good. *(Pleased at seeing* MASHA) Masha Ilyinishna!
MASHA. You know me? *(Grasps his hand.)*
TRIGORIN. Married?
MASHA. Long ago.
TRIGORIN. Are you happy? *(Bows to* DORN *and*
MEDVEDENKO, *then hesitatingly goes to* TREPLEFF)
Irina Nikolayevna tells me you have forgotten the past
and given up being angry.

*(*TREPLEFF *holds out his hand.)*

ARCADINA. *(To her son)* Look, Boris Alexeyevitch
has brought you the magazine with your last story.
TREPLEFF. *(Taking the magazine. To* TRIGORIN)
Thank you. You're very kind.

(They sit down.)

TRIGORIN. Your admirers send their respects to you.
In Petersburg and in Moscow, everywhere, there's a
great deal of interest in your work, and they all ask me
about you. They ask: what is he like, what age is he, is

he dark or fair? For some reason they all think you are
no longer young. And nobody knows your real name,
since you always publish under a pseudonym. You're a
mystery, like the Man in the Iron Mask.

TREPLEFF. Will you be with us long?

TRIGORIN. No, tomorrow I think I'll go to Moscow. I
must. I'm in a hurry to finish a story, and besides I've
promised to write something for an annual. In a word
it's the same old thing.

*(MADAME ARCADINA and PAULINE have set up a card
table. SHAMREYEFF lights candles, arranges chairs,
gets box of lotto from a cupboard.)*

TRIGORIN. The weather's given me a poor welcome.
The wind is ferocious. Tomorrow morning if it dies
down I'm going out to the lake to fish. And I want to
look around the garden and the place where—do you
remember?—your play was done. The idea for a story is
all worked out in my mind, I want only to refresh my
memory of the place where it's laid.

MASHA. Papa, let my husband have a horse! He must
get home.

SHAMREYEFF. *(Mimics)* A horse—home. *(Sternly)*
See for yourself: they are just back from the station.
They'll not go out again.

MASHA. They're not the only horses— *(Seeing that
he says nothing, she makes an impatient gesture)* Nobody can do anything with you—

MEDVEDENKO. I can walk, Masha. Truly—

PAULINE. *(Sighs)* Walk, in such weather! *(Sits down
at card table)* Sit down, friends.

MEDVEDENKO. It's only four miles. — Goodbye.
(Kisses wife's hand) Goodbye, Mama. *(His mother-in-
law puts out her hand reluctantly)* I should not have
troubled anybody, but the little baby— *(Bowing to
them)* Goodbye. *(He goes out as if apologizing.)*

SHAMREYEFF. He'll make it. He's not a general.

PAULINE. *(Taps on table)* Sit down, friends. Let's not lose time, they'll be calling us to supper soon.

(SHAMREYEFF, MASHA and DORN sit at the card table.)

ARCADINA. *(To TRIGORIN)* When these long autumn evenings draw on we pass the time out here with lotto. And look: the old lotto set we had when my mother used to play with us children. Don't you want to take a hand with us till supper time? *(She and TRIGORIN sit down at the table)* It's a tiresome game, but it does well enough when you're used to it. *(She deals three cards to each one.)*

TREPLEFF. *(Turns magazine pages)* He's read his own story, but mine he hasn't even cut. *(He lays the magazine on the desk; on his way out, as he passes his mother, he kisses her on the head.)*

ARCADINA. But you, Kostya?

TREPLEFF. Sorry, I don't care to. I'm going for a walk. *(Goes out.)*

ARCADINA. Stake—ten kopeks. Put it down for me, Doctor.

DORN. Command me.

MASHA. Has everybody bet? I'll begin. Twenty-two.

ARCADINA. I have it.

MASHA. Three.

DORN. Here you are.

MASHA. Did you put down three? Eight! Eighty-one! Ten!

SHAMREYEFF. Not so fast.

ARCADINA. What a reception they gave me at Kharkoff! Can you believe it, my head's spinning yet.

MASHA. Thirty-four.

(A sad waltz is heard.)

ARCADINA. The students gave me an ovation, three baskets of flowers, two wreaths and look— *(She takes off a brooch and puts it on the table.)*

SHAMREYEFF. Yes, that's the real—

MASHA. Fifty!

DORN. Fifty, you say?

ARCADINA. I had a superb costume. Say what you like, but really when it comes to dressing myself I am no fool.

PAULINE. Kostya is playing. The poor boy's sad.

SHAMREYEFF. In the papers they often abuse him.

MASHA. Seventy-seven.

ARCADINA. Who cares what they say?

TRIGORIN. He hasn't any luck. He still can't discover how to write a style of his own. There is something strange, vague, at times even like delirious raving. Not a single character that is alive.

MASHA. Eleven!

ARCADINA. *(Glancing at* SORIN) Petrusha, are you bored? *(A pause.)* He's asleep.

DORN. He's asleep, the State Counsellor.

MASHA. Seven! Ninety!

TRIGORIN. Do you think if I lived in such a place as this and by this lake, I would write? I should overcome such a passion and devote my life to fishing.

MASHA. Twenty-eight!

TRIGORIN. To catch a perch or a bass—that's something like happiness!

DORN. Well, I believe in Constantine Gavrilovitch. He has something! He has something! He thinks in images, his stories are bright and full of color, I always feel them strongly. It's only a pity that he's got no definite purpose. He creates impressions, never more than that, but on mere impressions you don't go far. Irina Nikolayevna, are you glad your son is a writer?

ARCADINA. Imagine, I have not read him yet. There's never time.

MASHA. Twenty-six!

(TREPLEFF *enters without saying anything, sits at his desk.)*

SHAMREYEFF. And, Boris Alexeyevitch, we've still got something of yours here.

TRIIGORIN. What's that?

SHAMREYEFF. Somehow or other Constantine Gavrilovitch shot a sea gull, and you asked me to have it stuffed for you.

TRIGORIN. I don't remember. *(Reflecting)* I don't remember.

MASHA. Sixty-six! One!

TREPLEFF. *(Throwing open the window, stands listening)* How dark! I don't know why I feel so uneasy.

ARCADINA. Kostya, shut the window, there's a draught.

(TREPLEFF *shuts window.)*

MASHA. Ninety-eight.

TRIGORIN. I've made a game.

ARCADINA. *(Gaily)* Bravo! Bravo!

SHAMREYEFF. Bravo!

ARCADINA. This man's lucky in everything, always. *(Rises)* And now let's go have a bite of something. Our celebrated author didn't have any dinner today. After supper we'll go on. Kostya, leave your manuscript, come have something to eat.

TREPLEFF. I don't want to, Mother, I've had enough.

ARCADINA. As you please. *(Wakes* SORIN) Petrusha, supper! *(Takes* SHAMREYEFF's *arm)* I'll tell you how they received me in Kharkoff.

(PAULINE *blows out candles on table. She and* DORN *wheel* SORIN's *chair out of the room. All but* TREPLEFF *go out. He gets ready to write. Runs his eye over what's already written.)*

TREPLEFF. I've talked so much about new forms, but now I feel that little by little I am slipping into mere routine myself. *(Reads)* "The placards on the wall proclaimed"—"pale face in a frame of dark hair"—frame

—that's flat. *(Scratches out what he's written)* I'll begin again where the hero is awakened by the rain, and throw out all the rest. This description of a moonlight night is too long and too precious. Trigorin has worked out his own method, it's easy for him. With him a broken bottle-neck lying on the dam glitters in the moonlight and the mill wheel casts a black shadow—and there before you is the moonlit night; but with me it's the shimmering light, and the silent twinkling of the stars, and the far-off sound of a piano dying away in the still, sweet-scented air. It's painful. *(A pause)* Yes, I'm coming more and more to the conclusion that it's a matter not of old forms and not of new forms, but that a man writes, not thinking at all of what form to choose, writes because it comes pouring out from his soul. *(A tap at the window nearest the desk.)* What's that? *(Looks out)* I don't see anything. *(Opens the door and peers into the garden)* Someone ran down the steps. *(Calls)* Who's there? *(Goes out. The sound of his steps along the veranda. A moment later returns with* NINA) Nina! Nina! *(She lays her head on his breast, with restrained sobbing.)*

TREPLEFF. *(Moved)* Nina! Nina! It's you—you. I had a presentment, all day my soul was tormented. *(Takes off her hat and cape)* Oh, my sweet, my darling, she has come! Let's not cry, let's not.

NINA. There's someone here.

TREPLEFF. No one.

NINA. Lock the doors. Someone might come in.

TREPLEFF. Nobody's coming in.

NINA. I know Irina Nikolayevna is here. Lock the doors.

TREPLEFF. *(Locks door on Right. Goes to door on Left)* This one doesn't lock. I'll put a chair against it. *(Puts chair against door)* Don't be afraid, nobody's coming in.

NINA. *(As if studying his face)* Let me look at you. *(Glancing around her)* It's warm, cozy— This used to be the drawing-room. Am I very much changed?

TREPLEFF. Yes—you are thinner and your eyes are bigger. Nina, how strange it is I'm seeing you. Why wouldn't you let me come to see you? Why didn't you come sooner? I know you've been here now for nearly a week. I have been every day there where you were, I stood under your window like a beggar.

NINA. I was afraid you might hate me. I dream every night that you look at me and don't recognize me. If you only knew! Ever since I came I've been here walking about—by the lake. I've been near your house often, and couldn't make up my mind to come in. Let's sit down. *(They sit.)* Let's sit down and let's talk, talk. It's pleasant here, warm, cozy— You hear—the wind? There's a place in Turgenev: "Happy is he who on such a night is under his own roof, who has a warm corner." I—a sea gull—no, that's not it. *(Rubs her forehead)* What was I saying? Yes—Turgenev. "And may the Lord help all homeless wanderers." It's nothing. *(Sobs.)*

TREPLEFF. Nina, again—Nina!

NINA. It's nothing. It will make me feel better. I've not cried for two years. Last night I came to the garden to see whether our theatre was still there, and it's there still. I cried for the first time in two years, and my heart grew lighter and my soul was clearer. Look, I'm not crying now. *(Takes his hand)* You are an author, I—an actress. We have both been drawn into the whirlpool. I used to be as happy as a child. I used to wake up in the morning singing. I loved you and dreamed of being famous, and now? Tomorrow early I must go to Yelets in the third class—with peasants, and at Yelets the cultured merchants will plague me with attentions. Life's brutal!

TREPLEFF. Why Yelets?

NINA. I've taken an engagement there for the winter. It's time I was going.

TREPLEFF. Nina, I cursed you and hated you. I tore up all your letters, tore up your photograph, and yet I knew every minute that my heart was bound to yours forever. It's not in my power to stop loving you, Nina.

Ever since I lost you and began to get my work published, my life has been unbearable—I am miserable—All of a sudden my youth was snatched from me, and now I feel as if I'd been living in the world for ninety years. I call out to you, I kiss the ground you walk on, I see your face wherever I look, the tender smile that shone on me those best years of my life.

NINA. *(In despair)* Why does he talk like that? Why does he talk like that?

TREPLEFF. I'm alone, not warmed by anybody's affection. I'm all chilled—it's cold like living in a cave. And no matter what I write it's dry, gloomy and harsh. Stay here, Nina, if you only would! and if you won't, then take me with you.

(NINA *quickly puts on her hat and cape.*)

TREPLEFF. Nina, why? For God's sake, Nina. *(He is looking at her as she puts her things on. A pause.)*

NINA. My horses are just out there. Don't see me off. I'll manage by myself. *(Sobbing)* Give me some water.

(*He gives her a glass of water.*)

TREPLEFF. Where are you going now?

NINA. To town. *(A pause)* Is Irina Nikolayevna here?

TREPLEFF. Yes, Thursday my uncle was not well, we telegraphed her to come.

NINA. Why do you say you kiss the ground I walk on? I ought to be killed. *(Bends over desk)* I'm so tired. If I could rest—rest. I'm a sea gull. No, that's not it. I'm an actress. Well, no matter— *(Hears* ARCADINA *and* TRIGORIN *laughing in the dining-room. She listens, runs to door on the Left and peeps through the key-hole)* And he's here too. *(Goes to* TREPLEFF*)* Well, no matter. He didn't believe in the theatre, all my dreams he'd laugh at, and little by little I quit believing in it myself, and lost heart. And there was the strain of love, jealousy, constant anxiety about my little baby. I got to be small and trashy, and played without thinking. I didn't know what to do with my hands, couldn't stand properly on the stage, couldn't control my voice. You can't imagine the feeling when you are acting and know it's dull. I'm a sea gull. No, that's not it. Do you remember, you shot a sea gull? A man comes by chance, sees it, and out of nothing else to do, destroys it. That's not it— *(Puts her hand to her forehead)* What was I—? I was talking about the stage. Now I'm not like that. I'm a real actress, I act with delight, with rapture, I'm drunk when I'm on the stage, and feel that I am beautiful. And now, ever since I've been here, I've kept walking about, kept walking and thinking, thinking and believing my soul grows stronger every day. Now I know, I understand, Kostya, that in our work—acting or writing—what matters is not fame, not glory, not what I used to dream about, it's how to endure, to bear my cross, and have faith. I have faith and it all doesn't hurt me so much, and when I think of my calling I'm not afraid of life.

TREPLEFF. *(Sadly)* You've found your way, you know where you are going, but I still move in a chaos of images and dreams, not knowing why or who it's for. I have no faith, and I don't know where my calling lies.

NINA. *(Listening)* Ssh—I'm going. Goodbye. When I'm a great actress, come and look at me. You promise? But now— *(Takes his hand)* It's late. I can hardly stand on my feet, I feel faint. I'd like something to eat.

TREPLEFF. Stay, I'll bring you some supper here.

NINA. No, no—I can manage by myself. The horses are just out there. So, she brought him along with her? But that's all one. When you see Trigorin—don't ever tell him anything. I love him. I love him even more than before. "An idea for a short story" I love, I love passionately, I love to desperation. How nice it used to be, Kostya! You remember? How gay and warm and pure our life was; what things we felt, tender, delicate like flowers. Do you remember? "Men and beasts, lions,

eagles and partridges, antlered deer, mute fishes dwelling in the water, star-fish and small creatures invisible
to the eye—these and all life have run their sad course
and are no more. Thousands of creatures have come and
gone since there was life on the earth. Vainly now the
pallid moon doth light her lamp. In the meadows the
cranes wake and cry no longer; and the beetles' hum is
silent in the linden groves." *(Impulsively embraces*
TREPLEFF, *and runs out by the terrace door.)*

(A pause.)

TREPLEFF. Too bad if any one meets her in the garden
and tells Mother. That might upset Mother. *(He stands
for two minutes tearing up all his manuscripts and
throwing them under the desk, then unlocks door on
Right, and goes out.)*

DORN. *(Trying to open the door on the Left)* That's
funny. This door seems to be locked. *(Enters and puts
chair back in its place)* A regular hurdle race—

(Enter MADAME ARCADINA *and* PAULINE, *behind them*
  YAKOV *with a tray and bottles;* MASHA, *then*
  SHAMREYEFF *and* TRIGORIN.)

ARCADINA. Put the claret and the beer for Boris
Alexandreyevitch here on the table. We'll play and
drink. Let's sit down, friends.

PAULINE. *(To* YAKOV) Bring the tea now, too.
(Lights the candles and sits down.)

SHAMREYEFF. *(Leading* TRIGORIN *to the cupboard)*
Here's the thing I was telling you about just now. By
your order.

TRIGORIN. *(Looking at the sea gull)* I don't remember. *(Reflecting)* I don't remember.

(Sound of a shot offstage Right. EVERYBODY *jumps.)*

ARCADINA. *(Alarmed)* What's that?

DORN. Nothing. It must be—in my medicine case—something blew up. Don't you worry. *(He goes out Right, in a moment returns)* So it was. A bottle of ether blew up. *(Sings)* Again I stand before thee.

ARCADINA. *(Sitting down at the table)* Phew, I was frightened! It reminded me of how— *(Puts her hands over her face)* Everything's black before my eyes.

DORN. *(Turning through the magazine, to* TRIGORIN*)* About two months ago in this magazine there was an article—a letter from America—and I wanted to ask you among other things— *(Puts his arm around* TRIGORIN'S *waist and leads him toward the front of the stage)* since I'm very much interested in this question. *(Dropping his voice)* Get Irina Nikolayevna somewhere away from here. The fact is Constantine Gavrilovitch has shot himself.

CURTAIN

NOTES FOR ACTORS

There is Chekhov and Chekhov. An actor in a production of *The Sea Gull* may have to contend with certain critical opinions that he hears expressed and that are undoubtedly true if we are talking about the production of some later play, where Chekhov has fully developed his characteristic method. But they are by no means wholly true about *The Sea Gull*, in which to a considerable extent Chekhov is related to the Continental drama headed by Ibsen. In such discussions a useful fact to recall is that *The Cherry Orchard*, Chekhov's last play, comes exactly eight years after *The Sea Gull*.

The title. Strictly speaking, the Russian of the title implies only *Gull*, which would obviously be doubtful in English.

Page 3, line 9. "The sun has just set." There are always differences of opinion as to how dark the stage should be for this opening scene. At one extreme are those who insist that, whatever else, we should be able to see the actors' faces. At the other are those who apparently believe the blacker the darkness, the bolder the realism.

Nemirovitch-Dantchenko, in *My Life in the Russian Theatre*, admirably translated by John Cournos, speaks of this search for reality by the young Moscow Art Theatre. "In this respect, at the beginning," he says, "we went too far. There were times, indeed, when the stage was so dark as to render invisible not only the actors' faces, but even their figures."

In this scene, as always, Chekhov, we must remember, sees his characters as inseparable from the world around them. "Nature, on her part," he says in one of his letters, "becomes animated if you are not squeamish about em-

63

ploying comparisons of her phenomena with ordinary human activities." During this scene, therefore, the day's mood and the hour, the lights, shadows and sounds must have a very definite creative importance.

Page 4, line 3. MEDVEDENKO. "Yes, the acting will be done by . . ." In this and other speeches of Medvedenko's the style is due to the peculiarities of the character, not to the weakness of the translator. I have followed Chekhov closely, and have tried to make the style characteristic. The schoolmaster is by no means a fool. He is a man thwarted by poverty, unrequited love, and his own lack of magnetism or persuasiveness. In a passage that Chekhov omitted from the final version of the play, this last trait is hit off to perfection: Medvedenko says, "The earth is round." "Then why," Dorn says, "do you say it so unconvincedly?"

Medvedenko has been brought to the point where he is apologizing, as it were, for his very existence, that is true. We should note, however, the extent to which he manages to be around, getting under people's feet, and keeps doggedly after what he wants. By the time the play is over, what with Constantine, when he can stand no more, putting himself out of the world and out of Masha's sight, and Masha free of the distraction of his presence, the meek Medvedenko is a good deal farther on the way to what he wants than most of the other characters.

Page 4, line 18. "I'd as soon not." Our own country expression, "I wouldn't care for any," is an exact translation of the Russian here. The negative of our "I should like"—"I shouldn't like"—does not convey the mild deference of Medvedenko's speech.

Page 4, line 19. (A pause.) Throughout the play Chekhov has indicated pauses. He has orchestrated, to that extent, all its scenes. These pauses should be noted as expressive in themselves, and not necessarily connected with what come after them. For a marked example of this—one out of many and providing a general comment on them all—we might consider the place

(ACT IV) where Arcadina turns from the card-table to her brother in his wheel-chair.

"Petrusha, are you bored? *(A pause.)* He's asleep." The pause thus written in is not connected with these two sentences that it falls between. And so far as they are concerned, it is not necessary. In itself, however, it can be made to convey a great many things, such things, for example, among many others, as the following:

Could those closed eyes mean death? Death coming thus in the midst of the patter of lotto! Is there a rush of memories in his sister's mind—their childhood once? And what tenderness might lie in her perceiving that he is only asleep, an old worn-out man; and that he is still only that little boy of long ago! Or he may be the image of all human fate, of her own fate—some day the bright head! et cetera—the melting eyes—the voice that has charmed thousands!

This is no mere excursion into sentiment on the translator's part; for through a brain like Arcadina's any or all of these reflections, both the poignant and the histrionic, might pass while that pause holds her.

To imagine the character's inner experience at the moment of the pause is, of course, to possess its content. The actor's problem is to project this content of the pause, or to have it so much within his inner consciousness that it enters into what he creates otherwise and qualifies his performance.

It is also true, in a subtle sort of way, that these pauses, as indicated, fit into the general scheme by which a kind of pulse of life is aimed at, a flow and ebb. The possibility that lies within a silence, a pause, with that overflow and then retreat of the emotion, and that cool settling of the idea, or with that growing sense of an emotion about to break forth, is a matter that should be kept in mind throughout Chekhov's scenes.

The pauses also provide a place for sounds from the outer world of nature, the town, the house, etc.

Page 4, line 26. (Enter SORIN—) Mr. Sidney Greenstreet tells me that for this entire rôle the time consumed in speaking his lines comes to seven minutes. You have perceived so much of Sorin's life and character that this short amount of time seems impossible. In the same way you would not believe after watching some of Chekhov's scenes that they are as short as they are, so much has been conveyed, so little said, and a good deal of what has been said was said in lines which, taken by themselves, might seem merely incidental.

With these Chekhov rôles it is as if their moments of action that we see on the stage were but tangents to the full round of their inner lives. It is as if they brought to the stage only a ripple of broken echoes from the life that goes on unseen by us as spectators. And by an interesting paradox, it is from this living, inner continuity, rather than from the actual, or even photographic, words and actions, that we get such a strong sense of reality in Chekhov, and are led to speak of his mastery of realism.

The actor's performance, therefore, must preserve an intense concentration while presenting an effect of the most natural and flowing relaxation.

Page 6, line 2. (Straightening his uncle's tie.) An example of a certain use of stage directions that Chekhov will exhibit from time to time in *The Sea Gull,* and will make a characteristic element in his dramatic technique. These stage directions can be distinguished from others in Chekhov or elsewhere by the fact that they are not meant to interpret the words. They differ from some piece of stage business that interprets or enhances the words, and that depends on the words for existence or point. The images they create are in themselves expressive. Thus they take the place of words. It follows, therefore, that they could not be deduced from the lines. A director, or actor, then, dealing with *The Sea Gull* must study and follow the text for this sort of stage business exactly as he follows it for the lines, and must make a distinction between this sort of stage business and the stage business that he himself invents. Constantine's straightening his uncle's tie says something that leads to the next remark and changes or qualifies the meaning of that remark.

Other examples of these images that exist apart from the words are the three or four pieces of business with Constantine's bandages in ACT III, and Masha's waltz in ACT IV. In their case a realistic image, some actual and recognizable action, is created to express some inner or complex thing for which Shakespeare would have created an expression in words. Chekhov uses such images to express the greater part of his full meaning, which in turn leaves him free to use the simplest and most likely sort of words. The realistic surface is thereby maintained without any such loss in inner content as the usual realism often imposes.

There is another point, however: an image of the sort we are discussing must not be mistaken for a piece of symbolism, which it is certainly not. Masha's waltz is an entirely different kind of thing from Chekhov's sea gull or Ibsen's wild duck. A symbol is not something that exists complete in itself, or that reproduces something that exists; a symbol represents something. But a stage image such as Masha's waltz is itself a reality, which amounts to saying that it expresses something.

Such images are, of course, an admirably expressive form of dramatic invention, but they are comparatively rare. Their very finality and completeness limit their frequency. We might list a few happy instances such as Lady Macbeth's sleep-walking scene—the greatest of all stage images perhaps—or Œdipus' entrance blinded; or Hippolytus when he puts on woman's clothes to deceive the bacchanti; or the sight of Lear wandering in the storm—an image still beyond the scope of stage mechanism and actuality, and still most certain of its effect when Shakespeare's words convey it—or the blind Anna with the masks from Troy, in *La Città Morta;* or, in American drama, the moment in *The Torch Bearers* when the widow, in all her crêpe and solemn black, cannot resist taking a curtain call along with the actors in

the Little Theatre play that her husband's death had
kept her out of.

Page 6, line 18. ". . . She recites. . . . Nekrasov. . . ."
The point here is that some of Nekrasov's lyrics were
regarded as models of "pure art," the perfect poetry
without ideas, about which a good deal was being said
in the decade of *The Sea Gull.*

Page 6, line 23. The *Fumes of Life,* by B. Markevitch,
first produced in 1888, at the Alexandrynsky Theatre, in
Petersburg, under the title *Olga Rantseva.*

Page 7, line 22. "Making a fuss over this novelist . . ."
It would be a mistake to conclude, as some have done,
that Constantine did not know of his mother's relation
to Trigorin. In the original form of the play that fact
was all to plain : Constantine says of Trigorin that now
he drinks only beer and loves only young women ; and
Arcadina says to Constantine, "I respect your freedom :
you too must leave me free to treat this man as I wish."

The censor required that the general presentation of
the relationship between mother and son be softened. To
that end various cuts, accordingly, were made by
Chekhov.

Page 7, line 37. "Kiev burgher" . . . this phrase
means nothing to an audience where there are no cate-
gories or graded levels of society. "Burgher" means
practically nothing, "common citizen" nothing. It may
as well be cut, both here and in ACT III, page 39, line 30.

For a different reason Constantine's allusion to his
father brings up the question of cutting. To shoot in a
reference to him like that (as a famous actor, etc.), and
do nothing more about it, would seem technically most
inadequate on the dramatist's part. The producer will
have to decide whether to cut it or not.

Page 8, line 4. ". . . what sort of man. . . ." Nemirovitch-Dantchenko has this note :

"During these years among Chekhov's intimate friends
was the new writer, Potapenko. He had come to the
fore with two tales, 'The Secretary of his Excellency'
and 'On Actual Service,' and immediately won a name.

He came from the provinces. He was very sociable, possessed an unusually pleasant, quick, sober intelligence, and infected and gladdened every one with his optimism. He wrote much and rapidly; he did not value his own writings too highly and made jests at the expense of his productions. He lived lavishly; was frank, simple, weak-willed; toward Chekhov he behaved affectionately and with complete acknowledgment of his pre-eminence. Women loved him passionately; above all, because he loved them and—chiefly—because he knew how to love.

"Many have thought that Trigorin in *The Sea Gull* is autobiograpihcal. And Tolstoi said as much somewhere. But I could never get away from the thought it was Potapenko, more than any one else, who served as a model for Trigorin.

"Nina Zaryetchnaya gives Trigorin a medallion, on which is inscribed a phrase from some story of Trigorin's—'If my life ever becomes necessary to you, come and take it.' This phrase comes from a story of Chekhov's, and it breathes of self-abnegation and simplicity natural to Chekhovian maidens.

"This has provided the motive for associating Trigorin with Chekhov himself. But this is mere coincidence; it is possible that Chekhov loved this strong yet tender expression of womanly devotion and wanted to repeat it.

"More valuable for the characterization of Trigorin is his relation to women; it does not resemble Anton Pavlovitch, but is closer to the image of Potapenko. In general, it is, of course, neither the one nor the other, but a combination of the two."

Page 8, line 39. ". . . a deputy who was . . . said . . ." What Chekhov really says is Assistant Procureur, prosecuting counsel serving the Ministry of Justice. The next grade was Procureur. Sorin was an Over-Procureur, with the title of Actual State Councillor, which, according to Peter the Great's *Table of Comparative Precedence,* ranks with Rear-Admiral and Major-

General. Producers who think their audiences likely to grasp the significance of these titles are fortunate; the terms I use are very unsatisfactory but at least practical.

To know these facts as to Sorin's rank and station, however, should keep the actor who plays the rôle from mistaking Sorin's candid self-analysis for homely provincialism, naïveté, or lack of breeding. It should also remind the actress who plays Arcadina, Sorin's sister, not to leave out the touch of *grande dame* that Arcadina must have.

Page 9, line 2. SORIN. "Strong but unpleasant . . ." is borrowed from Chekhov's general store of phrases; in the play Sorin says only "but unpleasant."

Page 10, line 1. NINA. "It's hard to act in your play." This is a good case of Chekhov's use of sequence—the mere fact of one thing's coming after another—as a medium of expression. Constantine has replied coldly to her enthusiastic inquiry about Trigorin, and without any apparent connection, her next remark is an objection to Constantine's way of writing drama. Three-fourths of what she is actually saying is not in the words at all.

Page 10, line 10. PAULINE. "It's getting damp. . . ." The actors in exploring this scene for the tone and so forth should note the way Chekhov brings together two kinds of love—the first, young, idyllic, shy, the second grown-up, clandestine, insistent—and uses the combination of the two and the transition from one to the other to express things he has not expressed in words. A good illustration of this phase of his technique.

Page 11, line 3. "*Accoucheur*" has good, salty point in this speech of Dorn's but is hard for audiences to hear or to understand. For women we have the word *midwife,* but for men bringing babies into the world we have no English word. In Dorn's case *doctor* may, though at a loss, prove to be theatrically more practicable, which means that the actor's tone of voice would have to further the meaning.

Page 11, line 11. SHAMREYEFF. ". . . ah, magnificent! Pure delight . . ." Shamreyeff, formerly a military man, now commands only whatever human beings, animals and strategy a country estate affords. But he has still a sense of authority, and a certain coarse formality and complicatedness appear in his speech. The actor will have to bear this in mind, or his lines will sound at times like merely awkward translation.

Page 11, line 14. "Take his Raspluyeff . . ." Sadovsky was a Moscow star who died in 1872. Raspluyeff was a low-comedy character in Sukhova Kobylin's *Kretchinsky's Wedding.* Shamreyeff's critical assurances are, therefore, meant to be absurd.

Page 10, line 38. "Why? In the relations . . ." Nemirovitch-Dantchenko records that Chekhov took pride in his profession, and speaks of noticing at Melekhovo, Chekhov's estate, eight hundred and some odd prescriptions on separate slips stuck on a nail. They covered a year and were for the peasants on the estate.

In this same volume are remarks on Chekhov's habits of work, his manner with people, his relations with women, etc., that the actor who plays Dorn might do well to look up.

Page 12, line 2. "Ladies and gentlemen, we begin! I beg your attention. I begin . . ." is in the formal tradition for opening a piece, as in *I Pagliacci*. It should be given in the mechanical-formal style, disconnected with the rest of the lines.

Page 12, line 7. ". . . show us what will be . . ." Here is a small device for stage uses that any actor would see. Something may be conveyed as to Chekhov's fate in translation by noting how the translations miss it variously:

(Koteliansky): "Two hundred thousand years from now there will be nothing."

(Editor, Rubin): "In two hundred thousand years there will be nothing at all."

(Fell): "There won't be anything in twice ten thousand years."

(Garnett): "There will be nothing in two hundred thousand years."

Chekhov says, in reply to what will be in two hundred thousand years, that in two hundred thousand years nothing will be.

Page 12, line 15. "Men and beasts, lions and . . ." Chekhov was in sympathy with the Symbolists, and makes Trepleff a young follower of the movement. The gentle satire here is also evident.

"The most hazardous thing in the play was Nina's monologue," Nemirovitch-Dantchenko writes. ". . . How would those words sound from the stage? . . . This monologue, which in the first performance at St. Petersburg had awakened laughter, which to such a degree is permeated with the lyrical mood of a real poet that in our production there could not have been the least doubt of its rightness and beauty, now resounded in the deep, tense silence and held attention. And there was not the shadow of a smile, not the least hint of anything untoward."

We are told that the actress playing Nina spoke the monologue in a kind of sing-song.

Page 14, line 5. SORIN. "Irina, my dear . . ." Chekhov has a much warmer term—"little mother." We have no equivalent for it to use in this speech; but knowing of it may color the actor's voice.

Page 14, line 37. MEDVEDENKO. "Nobody has any grounds for separating matter from spirit . . ." The rambling, ill-fitted style has been translated closely; it is Chekhov's for the school-master, and should be kept as such, not smoothed out in the fear that the passage may sound like a translation. Chekhov himself was interested in the life of country schoolteachers.

This speech of Medvedenko's is characteristic: the theoretical drift of the first sentence; the awkward structure of the second.

Page 15, 5. For the singing heard from across the lake, the Moscow Art Theatre in the original production of *The Sea Gull* used Glinka's *Temptation.*

Page 15, line 36. ". . . my dream. . . . But it will never come true." In the Koteliansky and the Garnett versions, Nina has to say that her dream "will never be realized."

Page 16, line 6. DORN. "I suppose we may raise the curtain. . . ." Dorn is sensitive to that shadowed effect, and is practical about clearing it up. *Frightening* is the literal translation, but the word as used here in Russian has an emotional weight that parallels our use of *awful* in ordinary conversation.

Page 16, line 17. "I love fishing." Fishing was Chekhov's own favorite diversion.

Page 17, line 13. ". . . unfortunate girl. They say her mother when she died willed the husband all her immense fortune, everything to the very last kopek, and now this little girl is left with nothing, since her father has already willed everything he has to the second wife." This is one of those Chekhov passages that translators can make sound involved purely by not sticking to Chekhov's text. I retain Chekhov's repetitions: *willed— willed, everything—everything.* I keep his balances: *mother—father,* and *the husband—the second wife,* and his gradation in tone from *girl* to *littla girl.* I use *willed* so as to keep the *is left.*

Mrs. Garnett's text is full of changes, omissions, useless fuddling of the pronouns, et cetera. "They say her mother left her father all her immense property—every farthing of it—and the girl has got nothing, as the father has already made a will leaving everything to his second wife."

Page 17, line 24. "Like having wooden legs." The translations vary from this to "bits of wood," "made of wood," "turned to stone," etc.

Page 19, line 27. "Let me talk to you." Nemirovitch-Dantchenko tells us that in the first version of *The Sea Gull* that Chekhov showed him, it was suddenly revealed in this scene between Masha and Dorn that she was his daughter. "Not a word was again said in the play concerning this circumstance. I said that one of two things must be done: either this idea must be developed, or it must be wholly rejected, all the more so if the first act was to end with this scene. According to the very nature of the theatre, the end of the first act should turn sharply in the direction in which the drama is to develop.

"Chekhov said: 'But the public likes seeing a loaded gun placed before it at the end of an act.'

" 'Quite true,' I said, 'but it is necessary for it to go off afterwards, and not be merely removed in the intermission.' . . . He agreed with me. The end was changed."

Page 19, line 13. "What can I do for you, child? What? What?" The Eisemann translation renders this: "I'm a physician, and there's no medicine for love or death." So much for what can happen to Chekhov among his translators.

Page 21, line 29. ARCADINA. "Beautifully dressed . . . praise her too much . . . bad luck . . ." Here as in ACT IV the meaning is to beware of too much praise if you would escape the evil eye, a superstition more familiar on the Continent than to our audiences.

Page 23, line 11. SORIN. "That's why you turn . . . that's why I turn . . ." The repetition of *that's why* (or *therefore*) follows Chekhov's pattern exactly.

Page 24, line 10. "What horses? How should I know —what horses!" The punctuation is Chekhov's and may affect the reading of this speech.

Page 24, line 31. (TRIGORIN *follows, with fishing-rods . . .*) Chekhov told Kachalov, who was studying the rôle, that Trigorin's fishing-rods "ought to be crooked, homemade, he makes them himself with his penknife. The cigar he smokes is a good one. Perhaps it is not an expensive one, but it must be in silver paper."

Page 25, line 26. "For the rest . . . stop hiding, stop pretending." This is Chekhov's order of words. In the essay on translating we have already seen the Garnett version. The Eisemann goes it one better:

"Let us at least not lie and feign at the evening of life."

Page 28, line 39. "At any rate, let's talk." Trigorin has been described by Sorin and Constantine as saying little and as reserved and melancholy. We see him now talking to this young girl, the only person in the play to whom he pours himself out. It is equally plain what the flattery of his confidences is working in her.

Page 29, line 7. "I must be writing." Nemirovitch-Dantchenko quotes Chekhov:

"Very shrewdly had Chekhov spoken of a writer of our own generation, Gneditch:

" 'This man is a real writer. There is one thing he cannot do: *not* write. Whatever conditions you surround him with, he'll take a gnawed pencil if he can't find a pen, and he'll take a piece of paper, and he'll write—a sketch, a story, a comedy, a collection of anecdotes. He married a wealthy woman, he has no need of earning a livelihood, and he goes on writing more than ever. When he's short of an original theme, then he takes to translating.' "

Page 29, line 36. "Writing at . . ." This is a close translation of the Russian diminutive form of the verb *write*, and carries here something pretty close to condescension.

Page 30, line 23. "I see it's not what I meant it to be." Chekhov said of *The Sea Gull* that he began it *forte* and ended it *pianissimo*.

Page 30, line 34. "What success?" Tolstoi said of *The Sea Gull:* "it is a trifle worth nothing; it is written just as Ibsen writes. He piles up things there, and why he does so you don't know." He considered the novelist's monologue the best passage in the play, but regarded it as autobiographical and hence better suited to appear elsewhere than in a play.

Page 34, line 4. "First he tries shooting himself . . ." In *Life and Letters of Anton Chekhov,* translated and edited by S. S. Koteliansky and Philip Tomlinson, will be found a discussion of the suicide motif in relation to Chekhov's own experiences as a doctor.

Page 35, line 11. (SORIN *in full dress . . .*) The costume that Chekhov directs for Sorin here serves at least five purposes. It emphasizes the social plane on which he belongs (a fact that involves Arcadina also and some of the others) and on which he moved the world. It provides an image of his putting on that world, as it were, before going back into it. It reminds us of the fact that Sorin's state of mind came not through any lack of eminence or station, but through his not having had the things he most wanted. It provides a contrast with Constantine's wretched clothes. It contrasts with Sorin's broken appearance in ACT IV.

Page 36, line 1. SORIN. ". . . gudgeon existence . . ." This phrase meaning *life without any responsibility* or *simpleton's life* is found in English as well as in Russian; but for theatre purposes another phrase might be substituted by the actor to suit his own case.

Page 38, line 12. "While I'm away . . ."
Arcadina says in Chekhov (literally): "But you are almost entirely healed. Is left a very nothing. But you with me away will not again do click-click?" Which is to say, "But it's almost entirely healed. What's left is nothing. While I'm away you won't do any more click-click?" (I wrote "any more" instead of "again" in order to keep Chekhov's design for the sentence, with "click-click" last.)

West: "It's nearly healed up now. Only the merest traces are left. You promise you won't do it again when I'm away?"

Calderon: "It's almost healed up. You won't be up to any of these silly tricks again, will you, when I'm gone?"

Garnett: "But you have almost completely healed. There is the merest trifle left. You won't do anything naughty again while I'm away, will you?" The first *you* is an instance of the elusive kind of havoc that Mrs. Garnett plays with Chekhov. When we strike this speech, we wonder for a second what's the matter, until we see that the trouble is with the idioms. If we hear "you have healed," we expect something to follow—"of your wounds," for example—and are unconsciously distracted by waiting for it and then not getting it. Otherwise our idiom, of course, calls for "It is healed."

Page 39, line 7. "developing Nina, trying to convince

her once and for all that he's a genius." This is an exact translation of Chekhov's words. They may not be attractive for Constantine to say, but they express his scorn, and they are sufficiently articulate to convince us of his gift for writing.

Page 39, line 3. "I myself . . . leave here." The literal is, "I myself beg him here (to) leave." Mrs. Garnett's version of this may serve, brief as it is, to illustrate the particular kind of harm she has done Chekhov by changing the form Chekhov used, blurring the emphasis, and ending up with a sentence hopeless for any actor: "It is I who am asking him to go."

Page 40, line 14. (TREPLEFF *picks up the bandage.)* Trepleff's stage business with the medicine cupboard and the bandage helps to cover Trigorin, so that we avoid a stark outlining of his scene. The ending of one scene occurs during the beginning of another. There are a good many spots in *The Sea Gull* where Chekhov does this interweaving. It prevents the single scenes, each so intense, from giving the effect of mere "numbers" strung together.

Page 40, line 22. TRIGORIN. "Why is it I felt sadness . . ." This sentence is, of course, fairly purple with sentiment that is very much dated. It could easily be written into our ordinary everyday terms; but if that were done, it would no longer be itself. Left as Chekhov meant it to be, it may be taken as an illustration of a certain fluent mediocrity in a highly gifted, popular author who, moreover, belonged to the nineties and, let us remember, has just been in contact with a young girl.

Page 41, line 12. ". . . carries us away to a world of dreams; on earth it alone can ever give us happiness." By merely placing the two phrases in such a relation, Chekhov partially expresses his thought. Note these four following translations and how none of them observes the arrangement. Only two stick to the contrasting words: *world of dreams* and *on earth.*

(Editor, Rubin): ". . . wafting me away into the

world of reveries, there is nothing on earth that can give happiness like that."

(Koteliansky) : ". . . which carries one off into a world of dreams—such love alone can give happiness on earth !"

(Fell) : "Love alone can bring happiness on earth, love enchanting, the poetical love of youth, that sweeps away the sorrows of the world."

(Garnett) : ". . . lifting one into a world of dreams— that's the only thing in life that can give happiness !"

Page 42, line 17. "However, if you like . . ."

Considering how she has torn his life up by the roots, dragging him around after her for years, this remark is brutal, perhaps the most ruthless in the play. It is also typical of that curious rapture of egotism into which temperaments like Arcadina's can fall.

Five of the translations change the "where" to "why" —"After all, why should you hurry?" One (West) retains the "where": "After all, where do you want to hurry off to?" But adding on the "you want" like that kills Chekhov's whole motif.

Page 46, line 33. The Russian expression that Pauline uses means literally, "Go with God." We have not that expression, and no matter what tone of annoyance the actress might use, the strangeness of the expression would thwart Chekhov's intention. "Go, if you're going to," seems, at least, to get the voice part of the speech well enough. The actor may prefer the literal.

Page 47, line 20. MASHA. ". . . and be always waiting for something, waiting for fine weather by the sea." There is a Russian expression, to wait for fine weather by the sea—where you may or may not find it—the meaning of which is obvious. In this sentence Chekhov has another of his word-patterns or arrangements: the word meaning *wait for* is not only repeated but the two identical words are placed together. You could get this by changing the *and* to *with*. The lines would then read ". . . let yourself go, with something always you are waiting for, waiting for fine, etc." That would at least convey the refrain pattern and the lyricism that Chekhov intended.

Page 47, line 28. MASHA. *(Waltzing silently a few steps)* "The great thing, Mama, is to be where I don't see him . . ." Meanwhile she hears him, and is drawn into his music as all of her is drawn to him. This piece of stage business must be one of the greatest images in the modern theatre. At least some turns of the waltz should be done as Chekhov indicates, without Masha's speaking. The remarkable completeness of this image will thus all the more appear.

Page 48, line 25. SORIN. "Where's my sister?" The audience should know without fail when Arcadina enters that she is not arriving but merely returning from the station.

Page 52, line 1. "You old Lovelace!" The Continental use of this name implies a Don Juan, a rake.

Page 52, line 28. TRIGORIN. "Your admirers send their respects. . . ." By having the two men sit down at this point, Chekhov makes a sort of dramatic unit of the scene between them. They belong to and yet are distinct from whatever else is going on there before our eyes.

Page 53, line 5. "Will you be with us a long time?" This speech puzzled me at first. I wondered, too, how an actor could ever manage to say it without getting a laugh; at best it might simmer down to our making allowances for some form of Russian naïveté. And yet it is clear that Constantine means well. Other translators, evidently, had felt this problem and tried to soften matters. Mrs. Garnett, for example, has, "Will you be able to make a long stay?" and Mr. Koteliansky: "Stopping for some time?"

The line, Надолго к Нам ?, means literally, "A long time with us?" The positive quality of *a long time* and the *with us* instead of merely *here* both show cordial intentions.

But once we take the scene in, and see what Chekhov is doing with the two of them seated there and trying to get through the awkward moment, Constantine's speech falls into place. The audience may laugh or not laugh, either way. The scene can take care of itself—the gauche, the pathetic, the loyal effort, the frustration, all contribute.

On the other hand, translations like the Fell or the Garnett distort the whole effect when they make Trigorin say "must go back" to Moscow. For him to come for a night and go back next day might have various implications that are at least unnecessary. There is nothing about *back* in the speech, which literally reads, "No, tomorrow methinks to Moscow."

Page 54, line 4. "When these long . . . lotto." In the evening at Melekhovo, Chekhov's estate, we are told, everybody played lotto.

Page 59, line 15. (Quickly puts on her hat and cape.) From the moment when Nina puts her cloak on and Constantine sees it and what it means, we have a descending pattern, as it were, that consists of the three straight, prose, practical speeches given him to say. It is on this decisive, final plane, though not without echoes of all the more emotional elements, that Constantine's tearing up of his manuscripts takes place. That is no mere flash-in-the-pan impulse: it is an acceptance and resolution. Chekhov means to clinch this point when he makes his stage directions call for the two minutes, with manuscript after manuscript torn up and thrown under the desk. The actor playing Constantine must understand and face this fact, and show us the decision and the deliberate, tragic finish that the destruction of the manuscript evinces. Otherwise all we get is a male-Nina exit to match the female-Nina exit that we have just seen. The rôle would thus lose significance. We should have merely the pathetic story of a sad young man, and should escape a large percent of the blunt and tragic issues that the conclusion of the play presents.